PAPER BOAT
IN
THE GANGA

WING COMMANDER
SRIKANTH BALAGANDAR

ISBN 979-8-89929-350-4

Dedication

To Lord Ram, whose presence guided,
And Sarayu, whose waters flowed,
To Lord Shiva, whose silence spoke,
And Vishnu, who made us whole.

To the Gods in Ayodhya's streets,
In Varanasi's eternal flame,
To Hanuman's strength and Lakshmi's grace,
Whose blessings we could not name.

This journey, *Paperboat on the Ganga*, we lay at their feet,
A humble offering to the divine light,
In their presence, we found the path,
And in their whispers, took flight.

Paper Boat on the Ganga

A paper boat is never meant to last.

Yet, in the fleeting moments before the water claims it, it lives. It rides the gentle ripples, hesitates at the edge of a current, trembles under the weight of a stray drop of water. It does not know where it is going, only that it is being carried.

Perhaps we, too, are paper boats—setting sail without knowing where the river will take us.

When we returned from Mahakumbh, we were different from the time we started. We shared our journey with many. Nearly a hundred people asked us the same question:

"You must have experienced a lot of crowd?"

It was the most natural question, one that came instantly, effortlessly. It made sense—after all, this was the Mahakumbh, an ocean of humanity converging upon a single sacred space. The crowd was expected. The crowd was supposed to be the defining experience.

But it wasn't.

The river had other plans.

When we set out, we thought like travelers. We made lists, booked hotels, mapped routes. We braced ourselves for congestion, for delays, for the overwhelming presence of millions. We were prepared for the rigmarole of the journey. But somewhere between the airport trolleys and the temple bells, between the hush of dawn prayers and the ringing of conch shells at dusk, the journey stopped being something to navigate.

It became something to be experienced.

The places did not merely exist on maps; they lived in whispers, in the dust of temple courtyards, in the rhythmic ringing of temple bells, in the silent prayers of strangers who stood beside us in the crowd.

In Naimisharanyam, an old man told us not stories, but truths—of places where gods walked, where battles were fought, where dharma was shaped not by force, but by choice. We listened, not as tourists, but as seekers who hadn't realized what they were seeking.

In Ayodhya, the streets breathed His name. Ram was not just a deity here. He was the pulse of the land. Even the wind whispered, *Jai Shri Ram.* The city did not demand devotion; it simply infused it into your breath. As we saw Lord Ram, he saw us too.

And then, Varanasi. The city where time does not move forward but spirals. Where fire never stops burning, and where every soul—king or beggar—finds the same sky, the same river, the same truth.

Prayagraj was not just a city; it was a confluence of forces beyond comprehension. The meeting of three rivers—the Ganga, the Yamuna, and the unseen Saraswati—was mirrored in us. Were we not, too, a confluence? The self we were before this journey, the self that watched in awe, and the self that would return— never quite the same.

When we started, we were travelers. Planners. Doers. We thought we were in control.

But the river had other plans.

A casual decision to shift our dates, a moment that seemed insignificant, may have saved our lives. The paper boat does not fight the current; it surrenders. And in surrendering, it finds its path.

By the eighth day, we were no longer moving forward.

We were being carried.

The journey was never about the crowd. The crowd is only visible to those who stand outside, measuring the experience by its weight in numbers. But when you step onto the path, something else happens. The path lays itself before you. The journey unfolds not as an obstacle, but as a revelation.

It was never about the destination.
It was never about the logistics.
It was about what the river had to show us.

A paper boat, fragile and fleeting, does not resist. It does not fight the current. It simply becomes the journey.

And that is what we became.

The Five Seekers

(From Left – Shashank, Arya, Ganapathy, Sabitha and Srikanth)

It was evening tea time, and as usual, our slack group buzzed with messages. A single tea cup emoji appeared in the chat, and within seconds, reactions poured in. It was an unspoken ritual—systems put on hibernate, chairs slowly vacated, and the office floor grew quieter. The shack across the road, our usual tea spot, was calling. Meetings were paused, deadlines temporarily forgotten. Whether it was tea or coffee didn't really matter; the point was to be there, to take a break, and to step away from the screen for a while.

The tea vendor, Yadaiah, was already busy—he must have been selling at least fifteen hundred cups a day. Someone joked that vending tea outside a corporate office was a better business model than working in IT. A few laughs followed. Conversations drifted from work to life, from trivial banter to deep musings. There was a comfort in these breaks, a rhythm to them, an unsaid camaraderie that made the long hours more bearable.

Sri—yes, that's what people called me. I was the go-to person in the office. The one people sought when things needed fixing, guidance was required, or decisions had to be made. My role as the Real Estate, Facilities, and Business Operations administrator meant I was always in the thick of things. There was a certain satisfaction in that, a quiet sense of purpose. It felt good to be counted on, to know that my efforts made things move forward.

Work had its demands, but it also had its moments of genuine connection. Helping a colleague navigate an issue, ensuring a smooth day for the team, or simply being part of an environment where people looked out for each other—that was what I valued most. It wasn't about authority or control; it was about making things easier for those around me.

Public speaking? I enjoyed it. Not for the limelight, but for the connection it created. Standing in front of an audience, sharing insights, engaging with professionals who were navigating similar challenges—it was fulfilling. I read a lot, prepared thoroughly, and always ensured I had something meaningful to say. It wasn't about being the center of attention, but about sharing something useful, something that might help someone else in their journey. Industry conferences, panel discussions, mentoring peers—it all added layers to my professional life that I deeply valued.

Beyond work, life was simple and good. Sabitha, my wife of twenty-eight years, was my anchor. A home maker by choice, she had built our world with warmth and laughter. We had weathered the ups and downs together, and through it all, our happiness graph had steadily climbed. Our son, Rishu, had recently stepped into the corporate world—a milestone that brought a quiet sense of pride.

There were the usual stresses, of course. Life had its share of deadlines, responsibilities, and uncertainties. But there was also contentment, a balance between ambition and gratitude. A job I enjoyed, a family I cherished, and a sense of purpose in both. That, perhaps, was all one could ask for.

Hey Sri, Sabitha called out, my cousin Ganapathy called and was suggesting whether we could go on a trip to Mahakumbh.

Is he mad, I snapped back. Does he even know that in those forty days Prayagraj have atleast forty crore people visiting. That was the previous kumbh count. God knows, this year it might even exceed. That is more than the entire population of Europe. You want to be at that place amongst the crowd. I am not really sure, I said as I was aimlessly browsing one TV channel after the other.

Just as I had finished saying that, her phone rang, here goes, she said. Probably Sri, Ganapathy heard you lamenting about the crowd. He is calling. She swiped the green button to receive the call as I noticed her shiny mauve nail polish. Hello, she said.

It was Ganapathy on line, is Sri there, he asked.

Sabitha smiled, ya ya, he is here pointlessly browsing channels not knowing what to see. You are on speaker.

Namaskaram, I said.

Ganapathy, switched the call to video and started. Look this year, seems to be special. It is Mahakumbh and seems it comes once in 144 years. I am sure, none of us would be alive by the time the next one comes, so let's at least discuss, draw a plan and see how it all would come together. Let's just do a paper exercise planning about the trip and see what is feasible. Going or not going is our next decision.

I thought, it was a fair point. Nothing wrong is drawing out a good plan.

This fellow needs a nudge from you Ganapathy, for things like this, he won't listen to us, Sabitha interjected.

I smiled, as Ganapathy continued.

Thala, you have been in North India for a fair period of time, why don't you just do that exercise. Plus you have contacts with a lot of people in that part of the country. I think you could come out with a decent tour plan.

Ganapathy's voice, was laced with a request mixed excitement mixed order type of a tone. Practically telling me to get the plan ready.

I nodded, smiling to myself, just as my son, Rish, walked in. He glanced at me and, with a wry look, snapped, "What are you smiling for? And how many times do we have to tell you to sit straight?"

I leaned back, stretching. "This is my house. I'm just relaxing," I countered.

"Posture," Sabitha remarked as she walked toward the balcony, already deep in conversation with Ganapathy. Rish followed her, shaking his head.

I adjusted myself, found a comfortable spot, and finally settled on a news channel.

Sabitha returned after twenty minutes, looking purposeful. "It's a good idea. Why don't you sit down and plan the trip?"

"You do it better," I said, hoping to pass the baton.

"Nope. This time, it's on you. If we go, I'll follow your plan. You are in full control of the itinerary. I'm just going to sit back and enjoy."

"Relax, it's just a plan. We're not even sure if we're going," I tried reasoning.

But her tone had already shifted into a relentless nudge. The decision had been made—I just hadn't realized it yet.

The next two days blurred into work and exhaustion. Early departures, late returns—there was simply no time to think about a trip. But then, on December 13, every news channel was flooded with coverage of the Prime Minister's visit to Prayagraj, inspecting the preparations for the Mahakumbh Mela 2025. He was set to unveil massive infrastructure projects worth a staggering ₹5,500 crores and launch an AI chatbot—"Kumbh Sah 'AI' Yak"—to assist pilgrims.

Spiritual leaders spoke about the significance of Mahakumbh, the confluence of the Ganga, Yamuna, and the elusive Saraswati. Triveni Sangam, the Akshayavat tree, and the very essence of Prayagraj were being described in poetic reverence.

None of this, however, particularly moved me. The religious aspect didn't hold my attention.

What did?

The sheer scale of planning and execution behind organizing an event of this magnitude.

Four hundred and fifty million people over forty days. That number alone was staggering.

What would it take to manage such an event? The logistics of feeder airports, rail networks, sanitation, power supply, food distribution, electronic surveillance, VIP security, and—most critically—crowd control. The complexity of coordination between government bodies, transport operators, hospitality services, and emergency response teams fascinated me.

The G20 Summit in Delhi had been a marvel in event execution, but that was controlled, sanitized, and focused on world leaders. The Mahakumbh was an entirely different beast—a chaotic, organic, free-flowing convergence of humanity on an unprecedented scale.

That was enough to pull me in.

I wasn't just planning a trip anymore. I was stepping into an immersive logistical puzzle.

With that shift in mindset, I finally sat down to plan. Drive? Train? Flight?

I called Ganapathy. "What's the best way to get there?"

His reply was sharp and final. "It's your plan. If you say we walk, we walk. Just plan it."

The call lasted all of fifteen seconds.

I muttered an expletive under my breath, only to find Sabitha standing at the door, arms crossed.

"No cussing while planning," she said, tossing me a knowing look before walking away.

Fine. Time to get serious.

I zoomed into a map of India, bringing Hyderabad and Prayagraj into view. Then, as I focused in further, places like Naimisharanyam, Ayodhya, Gorakhpur, Varanasi, and Chitrakoot started appearing. An idea sparked—why not make this a circular trip, starting from Lucknow and covering these places before ending in Prayagraj?

That felt right.

I opened an Excel sheet and got to work. After several iterations, an eight-day itinerary emerged—departing on 26th January and return back on 02 Feb.

When I briefed Sabitha and Ganapathy, something rare happened. Both approved with a small caveat that we postpone it by one week in view of the foggy weather conditions and possible flight delays.

I just made the date changes from 01 February to 08th February. And the plan was set.

Ganapathy even asked, "Bringing Rish along? I'll coordinate my side accordingly."

"Wait, I thought this was just a paper exercise?" I blurted.

Sabitha smirked. "What did you think this was? We're going."

Execution Begins

With the plan locked, Sabitha patted my back. "Now book the flights, hotels, and cabs."

I exhaled, picked up my phone, and sent a message to Aditya Loomba, a trusted friend in Delhi who ran a cab service. He immediately connected me to Aditi from Eco Rent a Cab in Lucknow.

Within twenty minutes, Aditi called. "Sir, my boss Aditya asked me to coordinate. Please share your itinerary."

That was fast.

I explained our needs—an eight-day road trip starting and ending in Lucknow.

Her response was confident. "This is what we do. Just send the itinerary and consider it done."

And just like that, a plan that started as a reluctant task had turned into something real.

I wasn't just arranging a trip. I was stepping into a grand spectacle—one that blended logistics, tradition, and an unmatched scale of human movement.

And this time, I wasn't just watching from the sidelines.

It was 29th January, when Aditi called to check with us for changes.

I saw her Whatsapp profile and she was a really young beautiful looking girl dressed in all red. Amazing profile picture I messaged back. Keep the smile and I bet you are an amazing resource to your company, I messaged.

She replied with a smiley and a thank you sir.

Just take care, that no one mistakes you to be a fire extinguisher. You look like one. I replied. Seeing that she was in all red.

Oh my god, she reverted.

We are set, Aditi….we should be at Lucknow airport around evening 6 PM. Would be nice, if I have the driver and vehicle details.

Sure Sir, we will have a driver allocated by 31st and the details will reach you. Since you are six people, we would be providing you with a carrier frame on top to keep your luggage too.

That would be fine and thank you.

News channels started flashing information about a stampede that happened at Prayagraj. Initially it started as some thirty members of the public injured while by evening it turned out to be a lot of deaths being reported.

Ganapathy, called, as per original plan, we should have been in Prayagraj today, he said. There seemed to have been a massive surge of visitors and something has happened. What should we do, he asked.

Meaning what, I snapped. We go as planned.

Arya was asking whether the whole trip would be safe, given all this.

Look, no place is absolutely safe. Not even your drawing room. It is all a mindset. Let's just go as planned.

No going back on our decision, no second thoughts. We just proceed, Sabitha said.

Rishab, came back from office that evening and said, he is having his senior leadership coming from US and the local boss wanted everyone to be available during the week. He wouldn't be able to take time for the entire week and be with us.

We had our first drop out. We did discuss possibilities, whether Rish, could join us directly at Prayagraj on the specified dates where we would be there and we could at least as a family take a dip at Sangam.

Two days is possible, let's check, he said.

We tried bringing Rishab, to Prayagraj directly or through Lucknow and the ticket prices for that only flight was trending at five times the usual cost. A round trip with stop overs to Prayagraj was costing close to a lakh.

That's too expensive said Rishab.

It's ok, if you have the intent to come, don't bother about the cost. Let's just do it, I said.

No, don't bother. He said.

I was feeling a bit troubled for leaving back our one son and he wouldn't want to come too.

Sabitha, signalled, let him do as he intends. Kumbh will come in future and we will ensure we take him then.

A thought ran in my mind, what were the odds of us going by the original plan and being caught in the stampede. It was truly high. A casual comment from Sabitha, made us consider a week's postponement and here we are seeing that tragic event as a news on TV.

A travel plan, that week could have easily pulled us to Sangam during the time and god forbid we could have experienced the stampede. Being in the city during that time by itself would have been tragic. As part of medical evacuation and crowd diversions and triaging of the affected many ghats would have been closed and things would have been chaotic for pilgrims that day. A casual comment about fog made us postpone the trip by a safer week.

Was that our first miracle.

A small prayer for the affected ones and we set out with our packing. It was just thirty-six hours and we were set to go.

Arya and Sabitha were on morning evening connects with both the ladies planning as to the things they want to carry. They discussed saree colour, nail paint and also visited the salon for a spruce up.

Ganapathy commented, Sri, these ladies don't seem to be coming for a spiritual tour. They have something in mind.

Sabitha, snapped….. while it is also a temple run tour, it is also a relaxed holiday environment. We need to ensure some upkeep done. Just some small things, a bleach, manicure, pedicure, facial, hair and brow trim and nail work.

Is there anything left…..Ganapathy said.

Sri and I are going to look like orderlies following you both carrying all your luggage, I guess. He said.

Guys, whatever you do, pack light I said.

We need to have sweaters and at least one dress each day and some sarees during temple visits said Arya.

Of course, still pack light, don't overload. Carry a laptop bag too so that we can take what is necessary when we go for river dips. I said.

It was the day of travel, Sabitha and I had our flight at 3 PM in which Ganapathy and family would be there.

I got a message from Indrajit that a very prominent publisher is in Hyderabad and wants to meet us at 10 AM at her hotel. Can you come, he said.

I couldn't miss this. Getting facetime with a publisher is a big deal and this one is important as I had three books ready and lined up for publishing.

Sabitha, was livid. Today is our day of travel. Why such sudden developments. Why can't he go alone and meet her.

Relax I said. Flight is at 3 and I will be back max by 11:30 AM.

She wasn't satisfied. She said, in case you get late, just reach the airport directly from there. We will meet there.

Fair point, I said. Will call, I said and left.

Mrs. Renu from Vitusta Publishing was a veteran in the publishing industry with a body of work unmatched in her space. The way she spoke about the industry and the pressures and changes the publishing industry was going through was insightful. She started with a word of apology for not having been responsive to our emails due to the numerous releases per month that were lined up.

We pitched our core idea about the two books that were ready and the third one in the works. She was impressed with the overall idea.

We heard those magical words from Mrs. Renu coming out. Sure guys, Vitusta would be keen to send you an agreement and we can take it from there.

It was music to my ears. A very thin veil of unnoticeable moist filled my eyes. No one could see it; I could feel it.

Mrs. Renu, dropped her car keys on to the centre table. It created a loud clang. I noticed Lord Ram's picture facing me from the key chain. I felt that he was looking at me and smiling.

We thanked Mrs. Renu and left. I was back home by 1130 AM.

Sabitha, gave me a gentle hug, when I told her what transpired. I was getting worked up for nothing. The fact of having a completely different activity when we are setting course on a trip made me uncomfortable. But it is really nice to hear the news. She said.

I was quiet throughout the journey from home to the airport. Sabitha, let me be. Probably allowing me soak into the beautiful news that I had received that morning.

Lord Ram smiling through that key chain making a publishing agreement possible on the day of travel when we were set to go to Ayodhya.

Was that miracle number two.

We landed at Lucknow Chaudhary Charan Singh airport at 0530 PM on 01ˢᵗ Feb.

It took a while for us to come out of Lucknow. The airport was newly renovated and well run. Not a big one but I must say a decent mid-sized one and well maintained. The rush was palpable. The number of aircraft bays and baggage carousel belts seemed enough and more. It took a while for us to get our bags and we slowly wheeled the trolley outside and I made eye contact with a smart tall uniformed man holding a placard with my name on it. A short nod towards him and he leapt forward to take over my trolley. I insisted on pushing my trolley and he then took over the trolley Arya was trying to push. Our Toyota Crysta was parked at a decent distance from the arrival terminal in the VIP bay.

Shobit took over all the luggage and began loading it at the carriage installed in the roof. Ganapathy was helping him out trying to lash it tightly.

In the meantime, my phone rang. Hello, I said, Welcome to our city, Aditi said from the other side. Wishing you all the best wishes for a happy next eight days and to have an amazing darshan in all the places including Prayagraj.

I thanked Aditi and we were set to leave.

A short discussion with Shobit to brief him on our destination for the day and our road trip commenced.

Lucknow to Naimisharanyam to Faizabad to Ayodhya to Gorakhpur to Varanasi to Prayagraj to Chitrakoot to Lucknow. This was supposed to be our plan. The route symbolised in the google maps was

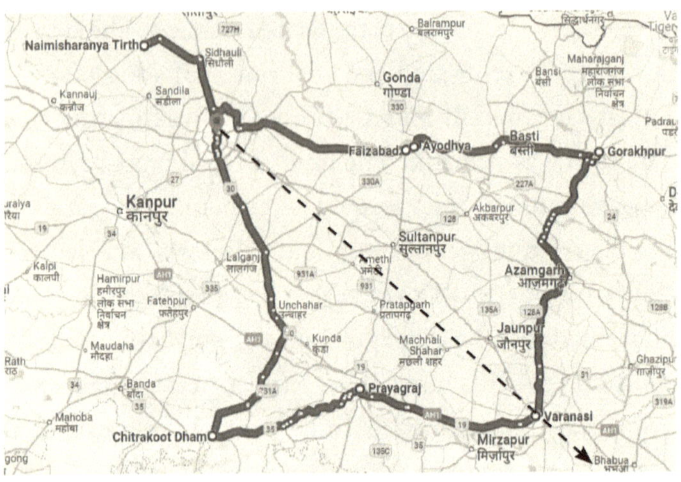

For an abstract artist the route appeared like a bow with its string pulled back. Gorakhpur and Chitrakoot appeared like the either ends of the tip of the bow. Varanasi resembled the middle and Lucknow was the point where the string of the bow was stretched to its maximum. The straight line drawn between Lucknow and Varanasi would naturally resemble an arrow. The entire depiction was Ram's bow in full display stretched to its full potential till Naimisharanyam.

Lucknow traffic was nothing to speak about, but the city, what a transformation. I had been there last in the year 1992 and since then what a change it has seen. The city is just beautiful with its flyovers, grade separators, traffic lights and broad roads. The new city was even better. Some traffic discipline from the population would just be that icing on the cake. With all the traffic jams and congestion, we slowly trudged our way to our hotel JP International at Naimisharanyam. A very backward tier-3 town. It was late evening and we dropped our bags and hit the only restaurant there which served dinner. There was no menu, there was a set menu and that was to be. We had a busy day tomorrow and quickly finished our meal and retired for the day.

The boy from the hotel knocked our room at five in the morning with tea. Temperatures were frigid at that time. Freezing to a point my fingers were numb. A hot cup of tea standing outside in the cold was beautiful. One could feel the fresh air with every deep breath, a rarity in our congested urban atmosphere.

A bearded old man, watched me from the ground and called me down. I walked down the stairs and addressed him with a namaste.

His reply was, Jai Shri Ram.

I must do that from now, I thought.

There are twenty or more temples all within a two kilometer radius of this place, I can take you to each of them. But your big vehicle will not go, you need to go in my Tuk Tuk, he said.

It was a cute makeshift jugaad innovation electric vehicle. The very sight of it made Sabitha and I wanted to travel in it.

Ganapathy and Arya were up and their son Shashank was idly wallowing under the quilt. The couple walked out, Ganapathy's teeth chattered and his trembling hands couldn't hold the tea without spilling the hot beverage between his fingers.

Arya, laughed out loud.

We just have the day at Naimisharanyam and were to be at Ayodhya that evening. We were all ready within the next hour and handed over all our luggage to Shobit to have it set in the vehicle and we commenced our visit to the temples in the town of Naimisharanyam.

The bearded aged auto driver, said, I can tell you all the stories of Naimisharanyam and we agreed. The man was in his late 70's and knowing things from a resident who has lived his entire life in the dusty lanes of this temple town would be good.

A guide in any place would generally speak as though he had memorised his script and would narrate it without a soul. We thought that would be the same with this old man. But what we heard was rather unexpected. He slowly went into a trance and chanted.

Om Shuklam Baratharam

Vishnum Shashi Varnam

Chaturbhujam Prasanna Vadhanam

Tya-yedhu Sarva Vignopashanthaye

Vyāsam Vaśiṣṭha-Naptāraṁ Śakteḥ Pautram Akalmaṣam
Parāśarātmajaṁ Vande Śukatātaṁ Taponidhim

Vyāsāya Viṣṇurūpāya Vyāsarūpāya Viṣṇave
Namo Vai Brahmanidhaye Vāsiṣṭhāya Namo Namaḥ

Sabitha and Arya, joined his chant while I listened with my eyes closed absorbing each line of the narration. His voice was like the ringing of a brass metal during the chant and his words, each one of them, seem to register at a sub-conscious level.

The old man took a deep breath, his gaze seemed completely different after the chant. It resembled Bhakti towards the sacred land of Naimisharanyam, as if absorbing its very essence. He then turned to us and began in a measured voice. "Naimisharanyam is not just a place; it is Prana itself, the very breath of life. Do you know why this forest is unlike any other? Because it holds the secret of the five life forces—the very energies that sustain all existence. Here, in this sacred soil, the ancient sages meditated and understood the rhythm of creation itself."

He closed his eyes for a brief moment, as if recalling something beyond time, then continued. "There are five vital forces—Prana, Apana, Udana, Samana, and Vyana. Each of these energies governs a part of your being, just as this land governs the cosmic order. Prana is the upward-moving force, controlling breath, thought, and perception, just like the trees here that reach towards the sky. Apana, the downward-moving force, is what grounds you, much like the roots that burrow into the sacred earth of Naimisharanyam. Udana, the force of expression, governs speech and consciousness, just as this land has been the birthplace of wisdom, where the Vedas and Puranas took form. Samana fuels digestion and balance, mirroring how this place harmonizes the forces of nature and spirituality. And Vyana, which flows everywhere, is the pulse of the universe, much like the Gomti River that weaves through this holy ground."

He looked at us, his eyes piercing. "This is why the sages chose this place. This is why Ved Vyasa compiled the Vedas here. This is why the very breath of the gods lingers in this air. It is not just a forest; it is the convergence of life's forces, a space where time dissolves and only essence remains."

We stood there, silent, as his words settled upon us like the first light of dawn. The air around us felt different now—not just air, but something alive, something ancient, something that had been whispering its truths long before we arrived. We were merely listening for the first time.

He smiled gently. "Now that you understand this, let me tell you the stories of Naimisharanyam." And with that, the journey into the heart of its legends began.

Naimisharanyam is in the banks of Gomti river and is one of the 12 Divyadesam that exists in North India. This Gomti river source is from the Himalayas and flows down east and mixes with the Ganga near Kanpur. Within that Naimisharanyam is the second place among the Divyadesams of North India and 97th in the total list. God is formless here, he is in the form of a forest here. We are about 75 kilometers from Lucknow. In the shastras wherever it is mentioned as Brahma vanam, Brahma sa vrikamaseeth it means Naimisharanyam is being talked about. The intent is to nudge humans to live and thrive as close to nature as possible. Sanatana Dharma is the only religion which recognizes that god is everywhere and all existent. Nature is God and Naimisharanyam is pure evidence to that.

Naimisharanyam is called so, because sages wanted to do a Yagna called Satra Yagna. Brahma then used darba grass and formed it into a ring, this ring went around and landed at Naimisharanyam. Naimi means the chakram and aranyam being forest hence Naimisharanyam. Another reason is that this place is famous for a special type of grass called Naimi and the forest of Naimi is called Naimisharanyam. Another way of seeing is Nimisha is a measure of time and a demon was killed within a fraction of a second in this forest and hence again Naimisharanyam.

When you read the original Mahabharata written by Ganesha and narrated by Ved Vyas the first line in the book goes like this

"Ugrasrava, the son of Lomaharshana, surnamed Sauti, well-versed in the Puranas, bending with humility, one day approached the great sages of rigid vows, sitting at their ease, who had attended the twelve years' sacrifice of Saunaka, surnamed Kulapati, in the forest of Naimisha".

I brought this out to let you know, that as Ved Vyas dictated the Mahabharata, Ganesha transcribed the great epic here in Naimisha. That is the belief here. However, there is another story that Ved Vyas dictated the Mahabharata to Lord Ganesha in the sacred caves of Vyasa Gufa located in Mana village near Badrinath, Uttarakhand. It is believed that Vyasa chose a secluded cave for serenity and Ganesha agreed to transcribe the epic under the condition that Vyasa would not pause his narration. In turn, Vyasa set a counter condition that Ganesha must fully comprehend each verse before writing it down allowing him time to composes the intricate poetry of the Mahabharata. Vyasa Gufa remains a revered pilgrimage site, where devotees visit to honor the place where one of the greatest epics of humanity was written. Whether the actual writing took place at Naimishe or at Vyasa Gufa, Naimishe is mentioned in Mahabharata at the very beginning.

Even in Srimad Bhagavatham the first line of the great Purana starts with

"Naimiṣe 'nimiṣa-kṣetre ṛṣayaḥ śaunakādayaḥ
satram svargāya lokāya sahasra-samam āsata"

Naimishe Animishe Kshetre—the sacred forest where time pauses, where the unblinking divine watches over, where seekers come not merely to witness but to listen, to understand, and perhaps, to awaken. These words are more than just an invocation; they carry within them the weight of eternity, the pulse of a sacred land that breathes with the whispers of sages and the silent watch of the divine. Naimishe—the very name conjures an image of an ancient forest, a place not merely of trees and earth, but of knowledge woven into the air itself. It is said that Lord Brahma, seeking a place where dharma could be protected and nurtured, released a divine chakra, a wheel that spun across the heavens and fell to Earth, marking this land as the holiest of all. Here, time itself is believed to move differently. A single moment in Naimisharanya, a mere nimisha, is said to be equal to thousands of years in the world beyond its borders. It is a land where sages gathered, where the first words of the Bhagavata Purana echoed, where the great epic of the Mahabharata was once transcribed. Animishe—that which does not blink, that which does not waver. In the language of the eternal, it is an epithet of Vishnu, the ever-watchful one, whose gaze never falters, whose awareness never dims. The word carries a deeper meaning, beyond divinity alone. It speaks of the sages who meditated in Naimisharanya, eyes unblinking, lost in the vastness of truth. It speaks of a realm untouched by the distractions of time, where knowledge flows like an unbroken river, where the soul awakens to something beyond the fleeting and the impermanent. Kshetre—not merely a place, but a field of consciousness, a space where the material dissolves into the spiritual. Naimisharanya is not just a geographical location; it is an experience, a portal where the sacred and the earthly merge, where those who seek find themselves standing at the threshold of something vast, something timeless. It is said that all the gods reside here, that every vibration of this soil carries the resonance of divine energy. Here, dharma was shaped, scriptures were spoken, and the whispers of the past continue to ripple through the present. To stand in Naimisharanya is to feel the weight of all that has come before—to breathe the same air where Vyasa compiled the Vedas, where Suta Maharishi recited the Bhagavata Purana, where sages sat in deep penance, their bodies still but their souls soaring beyond the confines of existence. The very air here seems to hum with an unseen presence, as if the space between each breath carries a story, a mantra, a forgotten truth waiting to be remembered.

I had a goose bump in my forearm as he said that. Mahabharata written at Naimisharanya and the first discourse of Srimad Bhagavatham at this very place.

Naimisharanyam is the only place apart from Patal Bhuvaneshwar where it is believed that all the 33 crore Hindu Gods and Goddesses reside. Since all the Gods, reside here, they all wanted to establish Dharma here. Dharma was born in Naimisha he said. But an asura named Vrittasur proved to be an obstacle. A great sage Dadhichi lived in Naimisha and the gods requested Dadhichi to donate his bones from which a weapon could be made to destroy Vrittasur. Dadhichi volunteered to donate his bones after all the gods appeared before him. He had a darshan of all the gods and after that his bones were used by Viswakarma to engineer Indra's mace which was used to kill Vrittasur.

Dadhichi Kund – Naimisharanya[1]

It is also believed that Ved Vyas compiled the six shastras, eighteen Puranas and the four vedas at Naimisha. Srimad Bhagavatham was spoken out loud at one stretch for the first time by Parashar to Raja Parikshit in one go.

Lord Vishnu killed Durjaya and Gayasura. His body was cut into three parts with one part falling at Naimisha and the other two falling at Gaya and Badrinath.

---

[1] *https://www.tourmyindia.com/states/uttarpradesh/dadhichi-kund-naimisharanya.html*

Nimisha means part of a second. It is believed that Brahma Mano Maya Chakra fell here giving the place its name. Nemi is the outer surface of the chakra. Naimisharanya is as old as time. It is believed that Satrupa and Swayambhu Manu who was the son of Lord Brahma performed penance 24000 years ago to Lord Narayana to be born as their son. They were blessed with two sons Priyavrathan and Uthanapadan. Priyavarthan had sons called Aagnedharan, Rishabadevan, Nabhi, Jatabarathan. Uthanapadan's son was Dhruva Maharaj. Apart from this they had three daughters Devahuti, Ahuti and Prasoothi. Devahuti married Karthama Prajapati and through them Sankhya philosophy came into existence. All this happened between Satrupa and Swayambhu Manu at Naimishe.

Lord Rama performed his Ashwamedha Yagna here to celebrate his victory over Ravana.

Apart from all this, there is also a story that Hayagriva imparted Lalitha Sahasranamam to Sage Agasthya here. Though I am not too sure about this, although it is also a story.

(Hayagrivar reciting Lalitha Sahasranamam to Sage Agasthya)

But the power of Lalitha Sahasranamam is so great that whoever chants it, all his accumulated sins will get destroyed, all diseases will subside, it is believed chanting it will avoid untimely death and remove pain caused by fever and confers longevity, goddess of wealth will reside in the house, one's power of words will improve and be a great communicator. For the concentrated chanter Brahma Gnana will be attained. It short chanting of Lalitha Sahasranamam helps in achieving what your mind is made out to be, ensures mental and physical health, ensures that one performs good deeds always, promotes happiness and joy within, offers a layer of protection, creates a positive environment, sharpens intellect, improves concentration, overcomes panic attacks, mood swings etc, brings harmony within the family and ensures overcome poverty and opens up the chakras leading to spiritual enlightenment.

Viswaroopam of Lalitha Devi

(Statue of Mahavishnu)[2]

[2] Source: https://spiritmeaning.org/benefits-of-the-potent-lalitha-sahasranamam/?srsltid=Afm BOorXSInYANi_1dtoV6RcEq5mR4u4dTxy_Cjoldp9wKgVdSRgxn38

This place is the only place that is mentioned in Ramayana which happened in the Treta Yuga and Mahabharata which happened in the Dwapara Yuga.

Naimisharanyam is timeless, stories go that the water at Naimisha is as holy as the water in Kailash Parvat, Mahavishnu's Parkadal. Lord Brahma is believed to have produced a ring out Darbha grass and advised the sages to perform penance at the place where the ring had fallen. The place where the ring had fallen down is said to be Naimisharanya.

This place finds mention in the Rig Veda, Valmiki Ramayana and also in the epic Raghuvamsham written by Kalidasa. It says

"Naimiṣaṁ prāpya munivara-vṛtaṁ
naiṣadhādhyuṣitaṁ ca"

meaning, "Reaching Naimisha, the forest inhabited by great sages and also visited by the Nishadha people". This verse describes King Raghu passing through the sacred forest of Naimisharanya, a place of great spiritual significance where sages performed penances and vedic rituals. It highlights Naimisharanya as a key spiritual center in ancient India.

Naimisharanyam is a spiritual hindu center of learning and a beautiful place for meditation.[3]

This is the beauty of Naimisharanyam and its relevance to Sanatana Dharma. I wanted to tell you all this before we leave our hotel because once we reach the various temples, it will be so crowded and traffic would be so heavy, it would be difficult to concentrate. Even this story, I don't tell it to everybody, I felt like you people are searching for something and hence I wanted to expose you to significance of this place so that you can continue whatever you are searching. He said this line, with a direct eye contact with me.

---

[3] *https://www.chardhamtour.in/naimisharanya.html*

It was like talking to me directly.

My eyes were transfixed to baba's eyes and I couldn't shake it off.

If you are all ready, we can start. He said, looking at me and nodding at me to take a seat next to him in the auto.

I thought, there is enough to experience in Naimisharanyam in eight days and we are here for a few hours with a set timeline to reach Ayodhya immediately after lunch. I sat beside baba as he steered his Tuk Tuk. Our shoulders touched frequently due the rocking of the vehicle due to the potholed roads. I could feel a rudraksha from baba's biceps touching me now and then.

I asked him to say more about Naimisha and he continued.

We are first going to Sri Lalitha Devi Mandir. You know Sati, wife of Lord Shiva, she immolated herself after which Shiva carried her body and commenced a tandav. On the way, her body split into 108 parts and it is believed that the heart fell at Naimisharanya at this spot. So we have Lalitha Devi Mandir. As he finished his narration, he slowly got the Tuk Tuk to a stop and pointed to a direction where we were to take to see Lalitha Devi Mandir. The door of the mandir was closed for a while for Shringar of the Devi and when it opened, it was a beautiful site to see.

4

A red band of cloth was given to Arya and me by the priest at the sanctorum. On our way out, Baba found us carrying the cloth and said, Jai Lalitha Devi maa…you got this cloth. It is very auspicious. Keep it in your puja room in your house.

Sabitha, immediately took it from me and secured it in her handbag. Ganapathy glanced at her and smiled. He will lose it, otherwise.. she said.

We reached Chakra Teerth next which is believed to be created by the disc emanating from Brahma's heart.

---

4 *https://www.prabhatkhabar.com/top-stories/naimisharanya-maa-lalita-devi-fulfills-wishes-of-devotees-she-is-second-in-108-shaktipeeths-know-detials-tvi*

5

The place has two concentric rings the outer ring is where bathing is allowed and inner ring is more secluded. For its significance I must say that pilgrims could maintain this place a lot better. A lot of small temples are all around this tirth and the place is extremely commercial. A quick visit and we were out of this place. But as a spiritual searcher, the crowd shouldn't bother you. The spiritual relevance is immense and you will find so many people in deep meditation in and around this place in spite of all the busy human activity around.

We will go to Vyas Gaddi now. The most important place where Ved Vyas narrated Mahabharat to Ganesha who transcribed it. Ved Vyas also worked on the Puranas, Vedas and Srimad Bhagavatham. Sukha Brahmam narrated the first Bhagavatham to Parikshit all this has happened here.

<hr>

6

6 *https://www.justdial.com/Sitapur/Vyas-Gaddi-Ved-Vyas-Gaddi-Naimisharanya-Naimisharanya/9999P5862-5862-18030307 0310-D8F3_BZDET/photos*

Shashank asked, where are we going next baba. Baba, looked at him and asked, son what are you doing.

Studying he replied.

Do well, you will shine, take some water from Dadhichi Kund and sip it. All your wishes will be fulfilled. You look strong and I think you do a lot of wrestling in an akhara.

Shashank blurted out laughing. No baba, just exercise in the gym not any akhara.

Baba smilingly, we don't have any gym in Naimisha. We have a lot of akharas here near Hanuman gaddi. Let's go he said.

What is it famous for, asked Sabitha.

The old man, got down from the vehicle to come to the section where Arya, Sabitha, Ganapathy and Shashank were sitting. I out of curiousness got out from the front area of the Tuk Tuk.

You must be knowing the Ahiravan story in Ramayana. The type of nods each one of us were doing each conveyed a different meaning. I did a up and down nod symbolising a "yes", I know the story. Sabitha and Shashank, nod was a side to side, symbolising a "no" to the story. Arya was a slight movement more from the neck than the head, symbolising I would love to hear the story and Ganapathy was something like a figure of eight, I know but I don't know.

"Confused character", I thought.

A few more devotees gathered close to us as the baba commenced the story of Ahiravan.

Beta, Ahiravan was the ruler of the Patalok where everything was upside down. He was the brother of Ravana. In the war, when Ravana's son Indrajit (also known as Meghnad) was killed by Lakshman. Ravana sought revenge and summoned Ahiravana from Patalok. Ahiravana was a master of dark magic and illusion, marking him a formidable adversary.

Ravana, convinced Ahiravana to capture Rama and Lakshmana and sacrifice them to Goddess Mahamaya. Vibhishan, learned of Ahiravana's plot and warned Ram. In spite of the warning and despite Hanuman's efforts Ahiravana tricked him by disguising himself as Vibhishana. He kidnapped Ram and Lakshman and transported them to Patalok. Hanuman vowed to rescue both of them and reached Ahiravan's palace where he was encountered Makardhwaja where the two engaged in a formidable battle culminating in Hanuman emerging victorious. Hanuman then fought numerous obstacles in Patalok and reached the palace to learn that the only way to defeat Ahiravan was to extinguish five magical lamps simultaneously. Assuming his Panchamukha Hanuman Form, with five faces representing different deities, Hanuman extinguished the lamps and confronted Ahiravana.

In the ensuing battle Hanuman slayed Ahiravana and brought back Ram and Lakshman.

So how, is it relevant to Naimisharanyam, asked Shashank.

Baba, smiled. Hanuman Gaddi which we are about to go, is the place where Hanuman killed Ahiravana. That battle took place at Naimisharanyam.

This place is full of stories from both these timeless epics, blurted Ganapathy.

Bhai saab, reverted the old man, there is an English word called mythology. One can say Greek mythology. But as regards India, all this is our history. These things actually happened. It is faith, it is history, it is our lineage and it is our culture. There is no doubt, Ram and Krishna existed and with them as avatars all they experienced is absolute truth.

He slowly went back to the drivers seat, mumbling let's go to Hanuman Gaddi now.

The historical happenings are so timeless, it deceives human mind to accept. But Naimisha provides so much of evidence. Mahabharata happened, Ramayana happened. All you need is to be here and experience it. Ram lives here, Hanuman lives here, Shiva lives here, Lalitha Devi Lives here, Brahma resides here, Saptha Rishis Atri, Bhrigu, Vasishtha, Vishwamitra, Gautama, Jamadagni and Bharadwaja all of them live here, every god in Sanatana Dharma live here. One dip in Naimisharanya means you have conversed with all the gods of Sanatana Dharma. This is not an ordinary place.

We drove around Naimisharanyam for another hour seeing the new Balaji temple which is more on the lines of Tirupati and other smaller temples.

I thought, Naimisharanyam is not a place that has a cluster of temples. It by itself is a temple.

We were almost done with the place as our Tuk Tuk slowly glided back to our hotel. Shobit was ready with all the luggage fully loaded and lashed.

Sabitha, Arya and Shashank went to the room for final checks when Ganapathy and I were talking to Baba.

Shukriya baba, I said. You patiently took us throughout the place and beautifully explained everything.

No beta, he said. I don't do it to everybody. Seeing you both, I realized you are here searching for something. That made me feel I should tell you the stories of this place. Naimisharanyam is not a tourist place. If you want to be here to just come see and leave, that is another story. But Gods live here and they themselves have stories to tell. All you need to do is to listen to the whispers of the gods. They just gave me an opportunity to convert that whisper into a voice and tell you.

Anyone who have heard these stories, have always come back to Naimisharanyam once again. I bet destiny will bring you here once again. If I am alive then, I will meet you. He said.

Arey baba, we will surely come.

For me, they weren't stories, they appeared like stoking a small fire. Every great sage of Hindu tradition has spent time in the soil of Naimisharanya. Saptha Rishi, All the Gods, what emerged from this place Vedas, Puranas, Shlokas, Lalitha Sahasranamam. So much from one place. That unsettled me.

This place is so rich in its history but still in descript to anyone. No bragging what it holds as knowledge in its coffers. Just silence with a firm belief that a seeker will find his or her way to the source.

Silence is often misunderstood. In a world of traffic and notifications and the chatter of conversations, silence can feel like a void.

True silence is never empty.

Like Naimisharanya.

It is the space where thoughts take shape, where emotions settle and where clarity emerges. Silence is a pause between words that give meaning. But in the world of chatter most of our words too have no meaning. Silence is that breath before a great decision, the hush before meaning, the clarity before knowledge. Silence is louder than the words that come out, a quiet stare, an unspoken understanding, the weight of a moment in stillness all those can communicate more than a thousand voices shouting at once. For those who dare to listen, silence is not the absence of sound, it is the presence of the infinite. A way to realize human consciousness.

Our Toyota commenced its journey as I saw Baba pocketing the wads of cash that we paid him for his service. For all others it was a payment for a service that he rendered us. For me it was something like a dhakshina for a guru who led me to realize what Naimisharanyam stands for.

I took one deep breath of the air of Naimisharanyam before our vehicle crossed the town's borders. The same air breathed in by Lord Ram, Hanuman, Ved Vyas, Saptha Rishi, Brahma breathed, Lalitha Devi, Saunaka muni and so many others. I felt a part of all of them inside me.

I could hear a voice inside me. It was the Sound of Silence telling me……. *"Come Back to Naimisharanyam"*.

I replied that inner voice loudly, "I will".

You will, what, Sabitha commented from behind.

Jai Shri Ram.

Our next stop Ayodhya.

Shobit slowly navigated the dusty village roads and joined the highway to commence the 220 kilometer journey. The road from Naimisharanyam to Ayodhya is more than just a stretch of asphalt winding through Uttar Pradesh's heartland. It is a journey through time, tradition and the soul of rural India. As the Crysta hummed along, leaving behind the sacred groves of Naimisharanyam, the landscape unfolded like a forgotten song, whispering stories of sages, rivers, and the rhythm of life untouched by the haste of modernity. Through Neemsar we passed where the air was still but it seemed that the hum of ancient chants could be heard as the road meandered past golden fields of rippling yellow mustard swaying like waves under the vast northern sky.

The gentle murmur of village life, cows ambling lazily, women drawing water from deep stone wells the occasional peacock gracing the roadside was like a soft but an unhurried melody. As Neemsar went by, Sidhauli arrived like an oasis of simple beauty, its small tea stalls and the fragrance of chai. A place where time itself seemed to be slow. Ataria followed where infinite mango orchards stood in solemn rows, their green canopy sheltering the land from the light winter sun, a reminder that nature in all its wisdom just nurtures without any expectations. It was Itaunja and Bakshi-ka-Talab was next. Old havelis resembling regal past and lakes reflecting the vastness of the sky holding the secrets of those forgotten ancient times.

Children ran barefoot and laughed loud and seemed to play all day. A rarity of site in concrete urban jungles. It was past lunch time and we had a quick bite for lunch at Barabanki. Some standard roti, dal and subzi in the roadside dhaba. Jai Shri Ram said the dhaba owner smiling at us knowing very well that we are going for his darshan.

Have an amazing darshan he said.

Ramji will bless you all. This road that is going to Ayodhya, is our itihaas. He bent down and touched the asphalt and with that he placed his right hand on his head.

Ramji has walked these tracks during his time. Keep him in your thoughts every second as you proceed to Ayodhya he said.

We were 12 kilometers short of Ayodhya crossing Faizabad and I asked Shobit to take a right turn into the cantonment. I had booked our rooms at Sainik Sadan at Faizabad. A cursory identification checks at the main gate and we were let into the army area. The Sainik Sadan was about a kilometer from the main gate and we reached the premises. Some army men, walked up to us and started helping us offload.

Located within the historic and spiritual heart of Ayodhya, the Sainik Sadan stands as a testament to the nation's gratitude towards its armed forces. The facility was inaugurated on 22 March 2024 by Lieutenant General NS Raja Subramani, this state-of-the-art transit accommodation is exclusively designed for serving and retired military personnel as well as their families. Located within the Ayodhya Cantonment near the Dogra Regimental Center, Sainik Sadan offers a serene and dignified retreat for those who have dedicated their lives to the nation's service.

The facility boasts of various two room cottages with each room have two rooms within it. There were seven such cottages each so appropriately named. We stayed at Room No 1 in Kishkinda. There was Lepakshi, Chitrakoot, Mithila, Prayag, Kishkindha, Hampi and Panchvati a total of seven such cottages.

At the center of the grand lawn, Maharshi Valmiki sat comfortably with his palmyra leaves. A beautiful sculpture so intricately worked upon that when one stands in front of the great sage, it appears the great sage is directly staring in your eye.

Valmiki reminds you to feel the whispers of the wind, the rustling of the leaves and the golden rays of the sun where the spirit of Ram Rajya lingers in the winds of Ayodhya. As you slowly savor the atmosphere, one can hear the distant scent of temple bells and incense, a peace that can't be put into words. The towering trees stand like sentinels giving home to the birds which keep chirping throughout the day. As you keenly listen one can hear the murmur of the Sarayu in the distance. The same waters which once borne the footsteps of Lord Ram himself.

Devour a silent moment alone in Sainik Sadan and you will realize that your mind recollects nothing else but the beautiful occurrences of the Ramayana. Vivid recollections of stories which your grandparents would have told you about the great epic. Lord Ram's character, Lakshman's devotion, Bharatha's sacrifice, Hanuman's strength and the prosperity of Ayodhya. Maa Sita in all her glory walked in these sands those days. You feel truly blessed.

I walked up to the reception and identified myself. Our two rooms were already fully set. I was greeted with a warm welcome by the courteous reception staff. The morning session at Naimisharanyam was both enriching and tiring. We all wanted a break for an hour. Shobit wanted to stretch a bit too. Frankly a shut-eye for an hour wouldn't hurt. By the time I reached the room after finishing the check-in formalities, the others had all hit the bed and taking their afternoon siesta. A faint snore came from the adjacent room.

I looked at Sabithatha, who is doing that. Ganapathy, Arya or Shashank.

Shut up, she said. As if you don't do it. Given an opportunity you will bring the cottage down with your snore.

I hit the bed and my eyes would have just closed, when the room bell rang.

It was one of the army staff looking for me. Jai Shri Ram saab, he said.

I reverted with a Jai Shri Ram too.

Saab, Subedar saab, has requested you to come to the reception. He said.

Oh sure.

It was Subedar Hukum Singh standing at a massive 6 feet 3 inches clad in army battle fatigues. He looked at me and braced up. Swagat hai saab, he said.

I replied with my brisk Air Force salute.

I see, you haven't requested for a darshan pass. What is your plan sir. That was a point blank on the face question. It meant bluntly, having come all the way, don't you want a darshan of Lord Ram.

That is when it dawned on me, that Sainik Sadan had a system of darshan special passes just like the way they have at Vaishno Devi.

A sort of a cold sweat ran in my body. Someone is calling me and asking me to apply for a pass. This is providence, I thought.

Saab, you should have asked for it a couple of days earlier. Still, as I see it you are likely to vacate only day after tomorrow. If you speak to the Commanding Officer he can help you with a pass for morning 7 AM darshan day after tomorrow (04th Feb).

I would be a fool if I don't give a try to this, I thought.

I walked up to Col Adit Saxena who was in his office. The officer was gracious enough to get up and receive me with a warm welcome. We sat for a few minutes and exchanged pleasantries over a cup of tea. Before putting up my request for the pass, I started with an apology for not applying earlier and I didn't even know such a thing exist. He was considerate enough to take all my details and assured that he would organize a pass for 04th Feb morning.

The administration need not have even bothered about organizing a pass for us. We didn't know and they could have, just let it be. One work less for an already overworked team out there. But they did and that changed everything. For a devotee, it was providence, something like Lord Ram enabling a pass for us so that we could see from a lot more closer quarters.

Right since the day we started discussing the trip, there is something or other that has been happening which is beyond the ordinary. Every happening was a voice or a handholding or a subtle assurance stating "I am there".

I went to back to Kishkindha and our Vanar Sena (oops….that included me) were all up and making small talk.

A good cup of tea would be amazing, said Sabitha.

Chalo, let's go to the restaurant and have a bite. It was a cozy small restaurant which had a menu offering that was more than sufficient to a Sainik Sadan resident. We ordered some chai and crispy onion pakoras. After that rustic temple run at Naimisharanyam and the long drive to Ayodhya, the bite of that crispy golden caramelized onion pakora was like mini Vaikunta. A bite of the pakora with a sip of hot tea, it was dance across the palate for all of us. The rising steam from the ginger cardamom chai was nothing but pure comfort.

As we relished the small eats, I briefed the group about the availability of Army special darshan pass for day after morning. The team was overjoyed hearing that.

I still wanted to take it with some caution. While availability of the passes would happen, I didn't want to miss attempting a darshan that evening itself.

I proposed to the group, that it is just around 04:30 PM and we could use the rest of the evening by going to Ayodhya and attempt a general darshan of Ram Lulla. Why not do that I said.

Ganapathy, said yes immediately. Others agreed.

I said, let's then leave in say 45 minutes and see how it goes.

I briefed Shobit to be ready for a departure in about 30 minutes and we all started to get ready.

We set course from Sainik Sadan towards Ayodhya. I had never been to Ayodhya ever. Every bit of information about the city was as a result of what I had read that resembled crumbling infrastructure. In stark contrast to what I had in mind, the city was just beautiful.

What a beautiful transformed city Ayodhya was. So befitting to Maryada Purushottam Ram. Any other way, it wouldn't have been apt to the Lord himself. One arterial roads lead directly to the Ram Janma Bhoomi site. Every shop, office or any commercial establishment had the name of Ram or a derivative of the name of Ram as the name of their establishment. Ram was everywhere. Even certain sweets in a halwai shop were named after

Ram, Lakshman or Sita. Ram was the very life blood of the city. Our vehicle meandered its way through the slow traffic, we expected some road barricades and diversions somewhere and it happened.

A police post stopped us and asked us to divert our vehicle to the left. No vehicle is allowed beyond that point. The temple was a full three kilometers from where we were. Shobit diverted the vehicle to the left and parked the vehicle at the Udaya Public School playground.

Sir, he said, I won't be able to go beyond this. He organized a Tuk Tuk for us here too.

Arya was delighted again, seeing the Tuk Tuk. Somehow, she took a liking to this cute vehicle.

The Tuk Tuk took us around for another 2 kilometers ahead and the driver informed us that this would be the last point and we need to walk from here.

It was 05:30 PM for us. We started our walk through the narrow bylanes of Ayodhya. Police diverted us whichever way we took. We just walked following the crowd. Devotees chanting Jai Shri Ram and the fervour increased rising to a crescendo. Every tenth house seemed to have a Ram – Sita Temple.

We savoured each moment of our walk, designer street lamp posts where another interesting one to see. Here are a few pictures of some interesting designs installed in those bylanes.

Prasad stalls littered both sides of some streets, making bulk sweets for distribution from inside the temple. Also to supply to sweet shops in the main market. Busy narrow alleys with commercial activity all in the name of Lord Ram. We could see and feel the prosperity in the town.

Our guiding north star to find direction to Ram Janma Bhoomi was the massive cranes at the main temple site. We crossed Hanuman Gaddi and Dashrath mahal. I got excited seeing Seetha ki Rasoi as I had read that a temple of such a nature is coming inside the premises.

Sabitha, nudged me ahead stating it is just another restaurant. Sita ki Rasoi inside is a temple. Just go on.

We reached a huge main market area. The road was well cordoned for pedestrians who were walking in both directions. Police ensured that the human traffic did not overlap. There was huge police presence and we followed the crowd to enter the premises. Crowd moved fast, at least police ensured that. We entered a premises where devotees needed to deposit all electronic items and their foot wear. With that having done and tokens collected we were ready to enter the main temple.

While I ensured that we all stayed as a unit and together, a different sort of an unexplained feeling was felt. My chest felt light and my thoughts were just about Ram as I walked behind the person in front of me. The queue snaked its way endlessly and it seemed never ending. We did our physical pat down checks at the main entry point and the line started again, but now we were inside the temple and in the last leg of our walk before we have the darshan of the Lord.

7

We climbed the first flight of stairs and then the second. The queue slowed down. For speed of movement, the queue was split into five files and amazingly well managed.

He was there, we could see him. I touched Sabitha's shoulder, she took my hand. I could see Lord Ram. Nothing else was visible, just him, just him, just him.

---

[7] *https://srjbtkshetra.org/*

Jai Shri Ram
Jai Shri Ram
Jai Shri Ram

The chants didn't sound rhetorical. It sounded like a person in need calling out to Lord Ram. His eyes as deep as the cosmic ocean, seeing beyond time, beyond devotion, beyond lifetimes. His smile bathed in the soft glow of lamps and the fragrance of sandalwood, Lord Ram was that bridge between what was, what is and what shall be. The central walls of the temple echoed ....

Yato Dharmastato Jayah

where there is dharma, there is victory and here in that sanctum, dharma has found its eternal home.

The crowd took small steps and it seemed to slow down and the line came to a halt. The curtains closed.

Sabitha, looked at me and said, looks like we are at the right time for evening aarti.

That feeling can only be experienced. Just goosebumps.

An old lady standing beside me, shouted, my Ramji, who is the god of all the worlds, didn't have a place to stay for 500 years. At last, he has his place now. She cried as she said this.

A man in tattered clothes and dust smeared all over his face and hands, all because of the torturous travel that he may have done, cried, all the hardships that I undergo is no match to what Ram is giving me today. His darshan during the aarti.

The bells commenced its ringing and vedic chants started as the curtains slowly opened. The head priest was passed the aarti and he slowly performed the aarti for Lord Ram. The crowd just stood there and watched. There was just silence. My eyes were just transfixed on Lord Ram. Nothing else was even visible.

---

[8] *Watermarked picture taken from India Today Instagram feed.*

I didn't know when I reached outside the temple sanctum. While my thoughts and sight were fixed on Ram, the crowd slowly took me out of the temple. It was the finest moment and the probably the only moment, I felt God.

The five of us were outside now.

Sabitha, came close and we held each other in a quiet embrace.

She looked at me. "Your eyes……tears", she said.

I blinked. A breath. A moment.

"I don't Know," I said.

We moved with the crowd and found ourselves in the main market. It was shopping time for the ladies, followed by dinner. We walked a lot, till we found a Tuk Tuk that would take us to Shobit.

It was near midnight, we reached Sainik Sadan.

That night, we slept in silence. Lord Ram was there – in our dreams.

The next day, we all got up a bit late. Ganapathy, Sabitha and I went for a small walk within Sainik Sadan premises. We spent most of the morning within the Sadan. We had an early lunch and then left the premises past noon. It was more of a touristy day. Visiting Hanuman Garhi, Dasrath Mahal and Mani Parvath.

This Mani Parvath was of significance and the place seemed to have more primates than humans. They were all over the place. This is the place where Bharatha shot an arrow at Hanuman with Sanjeevani Parvath as he was overflying Ayodhya. Bharatha seemed to mistake Hanuman as an intruder into Ayodhya airspace. Injured Hanuman seemed to have landed and met Bharatha and updated him about the ongoing war and took off again.

We attempted to stop at Naya Ghat where a diversion of Sarayu River was done. It was well maintained. But none of us had the mood for a river dip in that crowd.

There were too many traffic diversions and it truly became impossible for Shobit to navigate the vehicle within Ayodhya city. We decided to go back to Sainik Sadan.

We reached Sainik Sadan around 4 PM and after a quick round of tea, one of the reception staff at Sainik Sadan walked up to us and asked us to go to Guptkar Ghat which was just a kilometer from Sainik Sadan.

Saab, he said, Ramji at the end of his avatar decided to leave his paduka at that place and was never found after that. He is believed to have taken Jal Samaadhi there he said.

We immediately took the vehicle and were at Guptkar Ghat in the next 15 minutes. An hour of boating at Sarayu river. Wading in the same water which Lord Ram had. Sabitha, bent over and took some water in her palm and sprinkled it on all of us. We went spent some time on the other side of the river where the boat docked. Some fun activity was available, camel ride, turban tying and a few other play activity for children. The place was sparse in terms of human footfalls. That brought its aura. Professional photographers approached tourists nudging us to use their services for taking some pictures. It was a beautiful evening going on a boat on the Sarayu River.

It was twilight and the temple priests there were getting ready for the aarti of Sarayu.

After the aarti, Sabitha and Arya approached one of the vendors (by the looks of him that is what we thought he was). The ladies went to him and requested him whether he would have a lamp that they could light and set it afloat in the Sarayu.

The old man politely said, can you wait for five minutes. I will go and bring it. The man was back in no time and organized the lamp for both of them.

After some prayers, both Sabitha and Arya stepped into the Sarayu and set the lamps into the river. Both the burning lamps slowly started drifting into the river as the currents carried them downstream. We could see them floating till midriver. The old man, looked at Arya and stated, it is Lord Ram's blessing that your lamps have reached the middle of the river.

She enquired about him.

The old man, mentioned that he lived in Guptkar Ghat most of his life and claimed to have practiced yoga and meditation for the past twenty years.

We took leave from him with a namasthe.

Rituals were starting in one of the temples there. The temples require some serious renovation work. One priests along with his family seemed to live within the premises. He narrated how Raja Ram after his avatar took jal samaadhi at Guptkar ghat and along with him every living being in Ayodhya went along with the Lord.

As we walked out, we found, Sant Tulsidas song "Ramchandra Kripalu Bhajman" painted in the wall of the temple.

I have heard this song on youtube, Sabitha said.

The day seemed to be ending and we were on our way back to our room.

Shri Ram Chandra Kripalu Bhajaman

Harana Bhavabhaya Darunam

Navakanj Lochana Kanjamukh Kara

Kanjapada Kanjaarunam

May my mind pray to compassionate Shri Ram, the destroyer of the fears of life and death

With eyes, face and feet are like blooming crimson lotuses

Shri Ram Shri Ram

Kandarp Aganita Amit Chavi

Nav Neel Nirada Sundaram

Patapeeta Maanahu Tadit Ruchi-Suchi

Navmi Janak Sutaavaram

Glory to Shri Ram with boundless splendour exceeding innumerable cupids. He is like a newly formed beautiful fresh blue cloud. His yellow robe appears like lightning. The groom of Sitaji; daughter of King Janak.

Shri Ram Shri Ram

Bhaja Deena Bandhu Dinesh Danav

Daitya-Vansha-Nikandanam

Raghunand Anand Kand Koshal

Chanda Dasharatha Nandanam

I bow to the Lord of the Sun, friend to the needy, destroyer of demons

Son of the Raghuvanshi dynasty, who is bliss, Son of Kausalya and Dasharatha

Shri Ram Shri Ram

Sira Mukut Kundal Tilak Chaaru

Udaaru Anga Vibhushanam

Aajaanubhuj Shar Chaapadhara

Sangram-Jita-Khara Dooshanam

The one with a crown on his head, adorned with earrings, a tilak on His forehead, his body is decorated with ornaments.

He holds a bow and arrow and defeated Khar and Dushan in a fierce battle

Shri Ram Shri Ram

Iti Vadati Tulsidas Shankar Sheesh

Muni Man Ranjanam

Mama Hridaya Kanj Nivaas

Kuru Kaamaadi Khaladalaganjanam

Tulsidasji says O my beloved Shri Ram, the charmer of Lord Shiv, Sri Shesh and saints. please reside in my heart so that all my worldly desires and vices can be destroyed

Shri Ram Chandra Kripalu Bhajaman

Harana Bhavabhaya Darunam

Navakanj Lochana Kanjamukh

Kara Kanjapada Kanjaarunam

May my mind pray to compassionate Shri Ram, the destroyer of the fears of life and death

With eyes, face and feet are like blooming crimson lotuses

Sant Tulsidas

Sabitha played the song from her mobile. The voice of Suryagayathri sounded like a saxophone playing as the child sung the beautiful rendition.

We decided to be ready by 06:30 AM in the morning for our special darshan organized through the Army. The reception at Sainik Sadan confirmed that our passes got approved and they would issue it at 7 AM in the morning.

Arya and Sabitha ordered both Ganapathy and me to wear Dhoti for the darshan, while they planned to wear sarees. We were all ready at the stated time.

Activity at the reception was getting busy, the Army had a procedure to earmark a liaison officer to go along and facilitate the darshan for any family that was to carry out their prayers at Ram Janma Bhoomi. We were waiting for our liaison officer to come.

I was standing at the gate and a car came at a considerable speed and screeched to a halt. Emerged from within was a very dear friend Col Murthy and Mrs. Asha Murthy. In fact, Murthy son Hriday and our son Rishab were classmates from 8th standard and from that link our families became close. It was a real surprise to meet them there of all the places. The family was on its trip from Delhi and was at Ayodhya after finishing their Sangam dip.

Col Murthy stated that he had recently retired and was in his first leg of his re-employment and was carrying out the trip before he reported to his unit at Arunachal Pradesh.

I thanked him for his service and wished him all the luck.

As he came to know our plans to go to Mahakumbh, Col Murthy made a few calls and got our administrative work completed through the Army at Prayagraj. He gave me a point of contact and asked me to liaise with him for next steps. Frankly our dip at Mahakumbh at Prayagraj was finalized.

He gave me a full briefing about how to go about navigating Prayagraj and report to Saraswati Ghat and then go through the army for the dip.

A chance meeting and we get the most important information about how to go about our activity at Sangam and a smooth administrative work completed as we stood there at the gates of Sainik Sadan Ayodhya.

I didn't know what was going on. It was all sheer providence.

Incidentally both the families were allocated the same liaison officer and our convoy of vehicles left for Ram darshan.

Our route was skirting the city, going through Guptkar ghat leading directly to the last point till civil vehicles were permitted. It was a walk not more than a kilometre where a special area was earmarked for deposit of foot wear and electronic items. The usual security pat down checks happened and we walked to the temple for the darshan. We were taken through a special entrance.

Lord Ram was even closer this time. Just there, seeing us, seeing me, seeing Sabitha, seeing Ganapathy, seeing Arya and seeing Shashank. It was the closest one could get. Closer than a prayer, closer than a breath.

This time Sabitha, wept holding my hand as I wiped the corner of my eye. So did Arya and Ganapathy.

Col Murthy reached out into his pocket, pulled out a handkerchief and pressed it against his eyes.

Mrs. Asha, turned away, dabbing her eyes. Still one tear would deceive her and flowed through her cheek.

Not one among us was untouched. Not one left unshaken.

The Lord spoke to all of us in some way. A very very personal way.

We parted ways with Col Murthy and in a couple of hours we were on our way to Varanasi.

The Road to Questions

The wheels turned, and Ayodhya receded behind us, swallowed by the fading twilight. The golden hues of the early evening melted into deep oranges and purples, painting the sky like a forgotten hymn. The Crysta hummed steadily, gliding over the long, unbroken stretch of highway leading us towards Varanasi.

Inside the vehicle, a quiet lull had settled over the group. Ganapathy leaned back, arms folded, his eyes half-closed in thought. Arya absentmindedly scrolled through her phone, occasionally glancing up at the changing landscape outside. Sabitha rested her head against the window, the rhythm of the road lulling her into a light daze.

But inside me, there was no such stillness.

Something had shifted. Or maybe, something had been set into motion.

I turned to the window, watching the vast emptiness of the highway unfurl ahead. The road was straight, but my thoughts twisted and turned, looping back onto themselves, unwilling to settle.

I had seen Ram.

I had seen Him.

Not a sculpture. Not an idol. Not a representation. Him.

Even now, I struggled to grasp what that meant.

The rational mind—ever restless, ever eager to categorize, to measure, to dissect—tried to break it down. What had happened back there? What made that moment different?

I had visited temples before. Countless times. But this was unlike any other darshan.

The weight of devotion in the air, the chants of "Jai Shri Ram" rising and falling like an ocean tide, the collective energy of a people who had waited generations for this moment—was that what made it different?

Or was it something else?

I had stood there, transfixed, staring into His eyes. And for the first time in as long as I could remember, I had felt no need to think.

No mental analysis. No questioning. Just stillness. Just presence.

Was that faith?

I shifted slightly in my seat, exhaling slowly, as if trying to release the weight of the moment. I wasn't the kind to get swept up by these things. I was a planner, a man of logistics, of structure, of reason. But reason had felt irrelevant back there. The scaffolding of logic had crumbled under something far older, far deeper.

I closed my eyes briefly. And then, Naimisharanyam returned to me.

A place I had barely considered before stepping into it. A place I had assumed would be just another stop on our journey.

A place that refused to leave me.

That bearded old tuk-tuk driver—was he just a man earning a living? Or something else? He had seen something in me that I had not yet admitted to myself.

"You are searching for something."

The words had slipped past me then, dismissed as part of the experience. But now, as the echoes of Ayodhya still reverberated within, they carried new weight.

Had I come looking for something?

I hadn't thought so. I had believed I was merely traveling, experiencing, observing.

But what if I had been searching all along, without knowing it?

Naimisharanyam was unlike anywhere else. A land where epics were written, where the gods had walked, where wisdom had been whispered into the wind long before the world knew how to listen.

It was not a place. It was a presence.

Then came Ayodhya.

The logical part of me admired it. A city reborn, carefully planned, meticulously transformed, modernity embracing heritage. That alone was fascinating. But Ayodhya was not just a city. It was a heartbeat. It was a memory that had finally found form.

And then there was the darshan—the moment where past, present, and eternity collapsed into each other. I had expected to see Ram. I had not expected Ram to see me.

How could two places—so vastly different—both shake me at my core?

Naimisharanyam was a whisper, a hushed breath from sages who had long disappeared.

Ayodhya was a battle cry, a declaration of something undeniable.

And me?

I was neither a sage nor a warrior. I was simply caught between the two, adrift between knowing and not knowing.

Then why these moments? Why these small miracles that had begun to collect like scattered pieces of an unseen puzzle?

The stampede we had unknowingly avoided. The publisher meeting on the day of departure. The darshan passes that had been arranged before I even thought to ask. The old man's words in Naimisharanyam.

Coincidences? Or something more?

I had spent my life constructing certainty—approving plans, signing off on projects, making decisions that were clear, structured, and logical. But here I was, slipping into ambiguity.

And the mind hates ambiguity.

It craves resolution, finality, a verdict. But this—this was an open-ended question that refused to close.

The car hit a rough patch of road, jolting me back to the present. I glanced around. The others remained undisturbed. Outside, the landscape shifted—temple spires rose in the distance, villages stood untouched by time, farmers moved in slow, deliberate rhythm, as if working in tune with something greater than the need for urgency.

A strange thought crept in.

I am just a paper boat in all this turbulence.

What if these places weren't trying to give me answers?

What if they were just mirrors?

Mirrors that reflected the contradictions I carried within me—the part of me that marveled at planning, at structure, at logic, and the part of me that had stood before Ram and forgotten how to breathe.

Could both parts of me exist together?

Or would one have to bow to the other?

The car moved forward, but I remained in place, suspended in the quiet turbulence of my own mind.

I had no answers.

Not yet.

But for the first time, I wasn't sure I needed them.

Not yet.

Shobit called me out, Sir….your original plan had Gorakhpur in it. Aren't we going there, he asked.

We need more time in Varanasi, it is better we cut corners and go to Varanasi directly skipping Gorakhpur.

We did plan to go from Ayodhya to Gorakhpur, do the darshan of Gorakhnath ji and then on the same day reach Varanasi which may have been wild day. Skipping Gorakhpur seemed more sensible enabling us to enjoy the soul of the trip.

Shobit drove steadily as the miles between Ayodhya and Varanasi ticked down. The road stretched ahead, a mix of bustling traffic and long, quiet patches where only the hum of the engine filled the air. I was scrolling absentmindedly through my phone when a notification popped up.

Aditi: *How's the trip going?*

I glanced at Shobit, then back at my phone, then back at him again—this time with a stare so intense he must have thought I had just uncovered some deep, cosmic truth.

He raised an eyebrow. "What?"

I smirked. "Your boss just messaged me, asking how the trip is going."

Now it was his turn to smirk. "And?"

"And should I tell the truth, or should I lie?" I asked, tilting my head dramatically.

Shobit let out a loud laugh, the kind that makes you briefly question whether your car alignment is off. "You tell her whatever suits you best," he said. "Just remember—*you just had Lord Ram's darshan.*"

I gasped. "Are you implying divine intervention should dictate my response?"

"I'm just saying," he shrugged, suppressing another chuckle, "lying right after a spiritual experience might invite some… *instant karma.*"

I pretended to think deeply. "Hmm. So if I say we're having an *enlightening* journey full of *spiritual wisdom and deep reflections…*"

"Technically not a lie," Shobit nodded. "You did reflect on whether to lie or not just now."

I grinned and started typing.

Me: *Shobit and I are having a philosophical discussion inspired by Ayodhya. Deep reflections happening.*

I hit send and turned to him. "There. Now I just need to figure out a philosophy that justifies post-darshan highway snacking."

"That's easy," Shobit said, reaching into the glove compartment and tossing me a pack of chips. "Even Lord Ram spent years in exile eating whatever he could find."

I shook my head, laughing. "So, road-trip samosas are *prasad* now?"

"That," he said with a wise nod, "is between you and your conscience."

We drove on, Varanasi drawing closer, the road filled with laughter, philosophy, and the irresistible scent of roadside chai. The rural landscape slowly started turning more urban. More population, highway turning more into a city road, more traffic and more volume of shops and activity. Varanasi pincodes started appearing in the address plates of all the shops.

Varanasi is not a city. It is a paradox. A place where time has dominion, yet the clock never stops ticking. A land where shlokas are whispered into the dawn air as the horns of restless traffic scream into the same sky. A city where the sacred Ganga flows eternal, but the streets remain caught in the ceaseless movement of modern life. As we crossed Lal Bahadur Shastri Airport the duality of Varanasi unfolded. The drive through the city was a journey through layers of time – newly built highways coiled through fields that had likely seen the footsteps of wandering sages millennia ago. High-rise apartments and digital billboards competed for space against crumbling, ochre-washed havelis that stood as silent witness to history. The traffic thickened as we neared Cantt Railway Station where an ocean of people swarmed. Pilgrims with rudraksha in hands, students rushing past cycle rickshaws and tourists attempting to zig zag in the chaos with wide eyed curiosity. A temple town, a student town, a trader's town Varanasi was everything, all at once. Moving past the iconic Kashi Viswanath Corridor, the transformation was stunning. We were duly diverted by the police in view of the surge in tourist footfalls in the city. Pilgrims made it a point to visit Prayagraj and Varanasi as part of their tour. One goes all the way till Prayagraj, it would be prudent to make a trip to Varanasi too. That seemed to be the general trend. We were no different too. It is either Prayagraj first and next Varanasi or vice versa, but skipping one for the other was never to be. We were diverted many times and at some point, we were even doubtful whether our vehicle would be allowed till our hotel. Resourceful Shobit ensured he took us through those alleys. The interior alleys appeared as though the city was warped in time. It was a labyrinth that remain unchanged each one having its history of human civilization. After all it is believed the first settlers strolled these sands. We approached Assi ghat, the noise slowly gave way to the rhythm of the Ganga. The frenzy of the city dissolved into the serenity of the river. Time flowed differently here. It was the same river where saints had composed hymns where seekers found salvation where kings and beggars both surrendered their mortality. Finally, we reached Ravidas Ghat where we had our rooms booked at Hotel

Ganga Garden. Ravidas Ghat is the first of the eighty-four ghats of Varanasi. We checked in and the hotel staff had as requested allotted us rooms with the Ganga River view. Till the time we stayed, we did not want to miss a second of the grandeur of the great river.

Shobit said, sir…. While I can attempt to take you wherever you want. It would be best if you can take the Tuk Tuk for all your city trip. You just experienced the state of the city. If you want to travel in this vehicle, police will stop or divert us and you would have to waste a lot of time walking. It seemed a fair point. Shobit was practically free for the time we were in Varanasi. We asked him to relax.

(A view from our hotel)

An hour's break, Ganapathy, Shashank and I walked down to the reception. We wanted to take a briefing about the possibilities of visiting places given the huge surge in pilgrims.

Akhil, at the reception was a courteous young lad with ash smeared in his forehead with a dot of vermillion in the centre. Sir, whenever you visit Kashi, before you go anywhere you must visit Kaal Bhairav mandir first. After that only, you should go anywhere else. It is likely giving attendance. There is a lot of crowd there. Take a Tuk Tuk and you may have to stand for an hour in the queue before you get darshan. Beyond that I don't think you will be able to do anything much. By the time you finish and get out, it will be late and you would have just the energy to come back to the hotel.

It seemed a fair point.

Sabitha and Arya, walked down and after a brief discussion of the plan we all set course in the now famous Arya's favourite Tuk Tuk.

There was ear piercing noise on the roads, with every driver pointlessly honking their car or two wheeler or Tuk Tuk horns no matter what. It seemed to be a habit more than a requirement.

The shrill noise got into Sabitha and she howled at the driver, Bhaiya… at least you don't honk. Why do you keep your finger at the horn all the time.

She looked at me, with frowning her forehead… I am getting a headache with all this, she said.

Snaking our way through the alleys, streets and sometimes a busy road we reached the general area of Kaal Bhairav mandir after about an hour.

We were a bit famished and had a bite in one of those street side joints which Varanasi was so famous for. A city specialty called Malaiyo was quite enticing and my sweet tooth couldn't resist. One, two in and I looked at Sabitha for a third. She stared back, I understood.

Shashank had one. Ganapathy and Arya shared one. Sabitha was taking spoon fulls from each of us.

Hmmmm….. Malaiyo a winter dessert from Varanasi made by churning milk, infusing it with cardamom and saffron and topping it with dry fruits served in an earthen pot. Wah ….. never leave Varanasi without having one.

Tummy's full, we asked a vendor the location of Kaal Bhairav mandir. Just 300 meters from here he said. There didn't seem to be any queue. It was after another 10 minute walk in the narrow street, we checked with another shop about the location of Kaal Bhairav mandir. Just 300 meters he said. I craned my neck to see where and couldn't see much, another vendor with whom we checked said the same thing. The distance never seemed to reduce. After a while, we saw people queueing up. Relieved that the temple can't be far off, we joined the queue and then started our time in the queue. It was a slow-moving line but fast enough to cover 300 metres quickly. That 300 metres never seemed to get covered. The line snaked through streets, lanes, bylanes and at one point entered a house and came out from the other side. A human serpent uncoiling inch by inch. Human bodies moved left, then right, a synchronized pendulum of bodies adjusting to the tiniest shifts in movement. Shoulders brushed, feet shuffled, the momentum passed down the line like a slow moving ripple in still water. Within the congested environment where there was just place for humans to walk, we had frequent two wheelers passing by us. Not silently though, their honking would never stop. No one cared to move but the horns still blared. And finally we had Kaal Bhairav's darshan.

9

---

9 https://shrikashidham.com/shiva-temples/shri-kaal-bhairav-temple/

Kaal Bhairav a fierce manifestation of Lord Shiva adorned with a garland of skulls and holding a trident represents the destructive aspect of Shiva. Legends have it that Kaal Bhairav was born during a fierce battle between Lord Brahma and Lord Vishnu. Lord Shiva manifested as Kaal Bhairav to restore the cosmic balance.

As we trudged out of the Kaal Bhairav temple, our legs felt like they had been personally cursed by the deity himself. The only thing keeping us from collapsing on the sacred streets of Kashi was the thought of crashing onto our hotel beds—after a frugal dinner, of course. Our energy levels were at an all-time low, but apparently, that memo hadn't reached Ganapathy.

The man, who had been half-dead just minutes ago, suddenly sprang back to life after dinner like a phone that had been on 1% battery all day and just got plugged in. With a newfound burst of enthusiasm, he declared that he wanted to sit in the front of the tuk-tuk with the driver. Now, normally, this wouldn't have been a problem, but our tuk-tuk was already a tight squeeze. The driver was a hefty man, generously occupying most of the space, and to make matters worse, he had a co-driver—a guy whose only job seemed to be sitting there, nodding occasionally, and looking important.

So, there we were, watching Ganapathy attempt the impossible—squeezing himself into whatever little real estate was left in the front. It was a feat that defied both physics and common sense. He managed to wedge himself in, but with one butt cheek defiantly hanging out. If someone had taken a photo, it would've looked like an ad for the dangers of overconfidence.

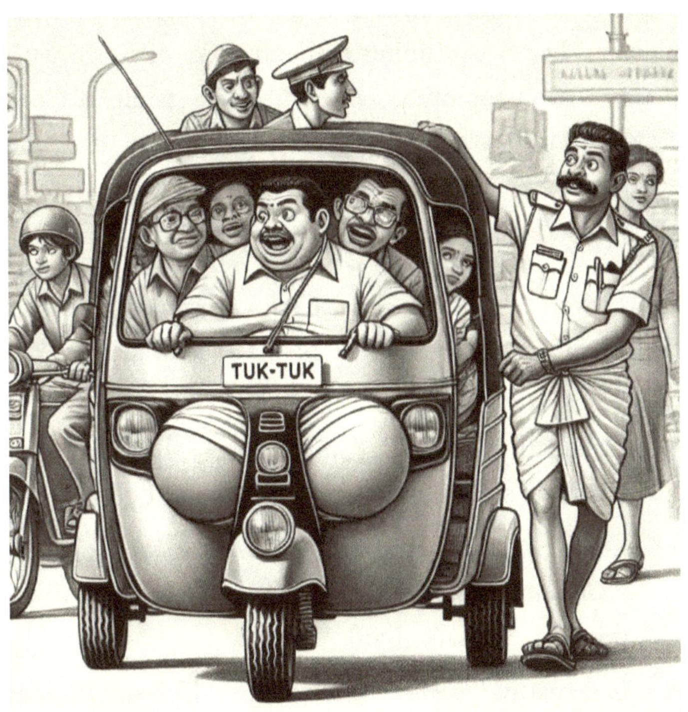

The tuk-tuk sputtered to life, and we, Arya, Sabitha, Shashank, and I, settled in the back, all of us curiously watching how this bizarre arrangement would unfold. It didn't take long for the real entertainment to begin.

Ganapathy, a proud Tamilian, did not know a single word of Hindi beyond "Namaste" and "Achha." The driver, on the other hand, spoke Hindi at the speed of a Delhi metro train, completely unaware that his front-seat passenger had no idea what he was saying. But that didn't stop either of them.

What followed was a legendary conversation—if you could call it that. The driver, completely in his element, began explaining the landmarks of Kashi with great passion, pointing here and there while his co-driver nodded sagely. Ganapathy, meanwhile, had one solid strategy—replying with an enthusiastic "Achha!" to everything.

> Driver: *"Yeh Vishwanath Gali hai, yahaan ka prasad bahut mashhoor hai!"* (This is Vishwanath Gali, famous for its prasad!)
>
> Ganapathy: *"Achha!"* (Translation: I have no idea what you said, but I'm going to pretend I do.)
>
> Driver: *"Yeh Manikarnika Ghat hai, yahan log mukti paane aate hain!"* (This is Manikarnika Ghat, where people attain salvation!)
>
> Ganapathy: *"Achha!"* (Translation: If I say 'Achha' enough times, will he stop talking?)
>
> Driver: *"Aage Ramnagar ka kila hai, aapko jaana hai?"* (Up ahead is Ramnagar Fort, do you want to visit?)
>
> Ganapathy: *"Achha!"*

By this point, we in the back were losing it. It was like watching a highly animated game of dumb charades. The driver was enthusiastically throwing in grand hand gestures, giving Ganapathy a full-fledged history lesson, and Ganapathy was responding like a broken chatbot with a one-word vocabulary.

Realizing that something was amiss, the driver finally paused and asked, *"Aapko samajh aa raha hai?"* (Are you understanding?)

Ganapathy, sweating profusely—not just from the heat but also from the sheer pressure of this unexpected oral examination—decided to take control. He turned to the driver and, in his best attempt at Hindi (which was essentially Tamil with English and vague gestures), said, *"Tamil... no Hindi. You know Tamil? Little-little?"*

The driver looked at him like he had just insulted his entire lineage. *"Nahin, bhaiya. Sirf Hindi."* (No, brother. Only Hindi.)

Not one to give up, Ganapathy now switched strategies. He resorted to a mix of English and exaggerated hand signals, like a man trying to communicate with aliens.

Ganapathy: *"Temple... you know? Shiva... Bhairav... big-big... many-many people!"* (Vigorous hand gestures as if sculpting an invisible temple in the air.)

Driver: *"Haan bhaiya!"* (Yes, brother!)

Ganapathy: *"We... go hotel. Fast-fast!"* (Now making rapid forward-driving motions with his hands.)

Driver: *"Haan bhaiya!"* (Yes, brother!)

By now, we were doubled over in laughter in the back. It was as if two people from completely different planets were trying to have a deep, philosophical discussion.

Sabitha whispered, "I think he's sweating more from this conversation than from almost falling out of the tuk-tuk."

Shashank added, "Forget the hotel; this ride alone is the highlight of the trip."

Meanwhile, Ganapathy, still bravely struggling, suddenly turned back to us and hissed, *"Dei, say something!"*

But we were far too entertained to intervene.

The driver, oblivious to our suffering, continued with his Hindi commentary, and Ganapathy, now completely exhausted, had resigned himself to nodding like a man who had accepted his fate. The ride finally came to an end, and as Ganapathy climbed out—one butt cheek at a time—he looked at us, drenched in sweat, and groaned, "Next time, someone else sit in the front."

Arya patted him on the back. "Good job, man. You just passed Level 1 Hindi."

Sabitha laughed, "And you've officially been accepted into the International Dumb Charades Championship."

As we walked into the hotel, still giggling over what had just transpired, Ganapathy shook his head, muttering, "Achha! Achha! That's all I'll ever need to know in Hindi."

And with that, we called it a night.

The darshan at Kaal Bhairav the previous day was a point of caution given the huge crowd at places of workship at Varanasi. Some doubts lingered in our mind, whether this was the right time.

Ganapathy said, there is no wrong time to come. We are here and we shall finish it, he said.

That was a catalyst for all of us to take briefing from Akhil again.

We hired a boat from the jetty. The boatman, a young boy named Nilesh came and shook hands with me. Sir Akhil has asked to take you from here till Namo Ghat. Ravidas Ghat was the 1st ghat and Namo Ghat is the 84th. After that I will drop you near Manikarnika Ghat and you can walk down to have a darshan of Kashi Vishwanath.

One request sir, this person here, is Panditji at Kashi Vishwanath temple. He is requesting whether he can join you and he would get down at Manikarnika ghat and go for his duty at Kashi Vishwanath.

A middle aged young smart looking man but who carried the aura of someone much older. A person who has seen time not in years but in prayers. His crisp saffron dhoti and neatly draped angavastram were spotless, the fabric carrying a sense of temple incense. His face was sharp, well defined with its deep-set eyes which held the weight of both scriptures. His forehead bore the traditional tripundra, perfectly drawn with sacred ash and his fingers had the faint smudges of Kumkum and

Vibhuti, the imprint of countless arti's performed at the sanctum.

None of us could say a no to him.

Sabitha, talked to him warmly, please come over Panditji she said.

He quickly got into the boat and settled himself into one corner.

Nilesh started the motor and the gave the boat its initial push and we were off into the mighty Ganga setting sail looking at each of the ghat and its grandeur viewing each one from the river.

The boat rocks gently as it leaves Ravidas Ghat, cutting through the golden morning sunlight shimmering on the Ganga's rippling surface. The city of Kashi awakens. Temple bell chime in the distance, conches blow and the air carries the fragrance of marigold, incense and faint wood smoke from unseen rituals. Panditji sitting cross legged near the bow, tilts his face to the sky as if listening to something beyond the senses.

Sabitha, walks up to him and requests whether he could tell us all about the significance of Kashi.

Panditji smiled a bit and turned towards us with a namaste. This is Kashi, what exists nowhere else, exists here. And is here, cannot be found anywhere else. He dips his fingers into the river, watching the droplets slip back into the sacred waters. This is not water – it is time itself, flowing circling back, dissolving, yet remaining untouched. The Ganga does not flow; she liberates. Every morning when the sun touches her waves, thousands awaken from the darkness of ignorance into the light of realization. And at night, when the lamps drift on her surface, they are not just flames – they are prayers, they are lives, they are whispers of those who have walked this path before us. Kashi is not a city. It is a living being. And the Ghats – these steps leading down the river – are its breath. Each ghat is a doorway, a question, a lesson. Some speak of creation, others of destruction. Some whisper of renunciation, others of celebration. But all, in the lead to one truth – that here in Kashi, the cycle of life and death does not bind you, it frees you.

There is a saying in ancient Hindu scriptures: he who dies in Varanasi attains liberation. The belief has drawn countless souls to this sacred city for centuries, yearning not for mere heaven, but for something far greater—the escape from the unending cycle of birth and rebirth. Yet, like all great truths, this too has a hidden layer, waiting to be unravelled. Varanasi. The name rolls off the tongue like the gentle waves of the Ganges lapping against its ghats. The city of Shiva, the eternal cosmic dancer, where time itself seems to pause and watch. The air is thick with the scent of burning incense, mingling with the distant hum of temple bells and the rhythmic chants of sadhus wrapped in saffron. Every brick, every step, every gaze carries the weight of ancient wisdom. And yet, the true Varanasi does not reside in its narrow alleys or its towering temples. No, Varanasi is something far deeper. It is not a place; it is a state of being. In Sanskrit, 'Varana' means eyebrows, and 'Nasi' means nose. The two converge at a single point—the space where the third eye resides, the gateway to inner vision. To die in Varanasi is not merely to breathe one's last in the city by the river, but to awaken the inner sight, to reside in the third eye. It is the journey from the ordinary vision of the world to the extraordinary vision of truth. It is to step beyond illusion, beyond the veils of desires and fears, into the space where existence is seen for what it truly is. Imagine this: You begin at the root, bound by the weight of survival, shackled to the cravings of the body—the hunger for food, the thirst for power, the ceaseless game of wanting and acquiring. The world here is dense, slow, heavy. You climb upward, shifting through the turbulence of emotions, the wavering tides of love and loss, the fire of ambition, the cold touch of rejection. Still, you ascend. Higher, through the gateway of expression, purifying every word, every breath, every silence. And then, if you are willing, if you are ready, you rise further.

Here, in the space of the third eye, the world no longer presses in on you; it expands outward. The noise fades, and in its place comes a stillness so profound it seems to hum with the whisper of the cosmos. This is the true Varanasi—the place where trust is not a decision but an existence, where contentment is not pursued but lived, where faith is not blind but all-seeing. Here, you do not seek goodness; you become it. Not as an act, but as a state. To bring your energy to the third eye is the greatest pilgrimage a human can undertake. Not one that involves weary steps through the dust-laden paths of the physical world, but one that moves through the corridors of the self, shedding layers of falsehood, reaching toward clarity. It is the crossing over, the release, the final arrival at the true home. So, when the ancients spoke of dying in Varanasi, they did not mean the mere cessation of breath in a city of stone and river. They meant the death of the lesser self, the dissolution of illusion, the merging into truth. They meant the awakening into the infinite. To reside in Varanasi is not to live in a city; it is to live in a state of being where the third eye opens, and one sees—not with the eyes of the body, but with the vision of the soul.

The boat glides past the first stretch of ghats, their stone steps *worn smooth by time, the air thick with the songs of sages, the silent grief of the mourning, the joyous cries of children splashing in the holy waters. Panditji watches the scene unfold before him, his eyes reflecting the city's eternal dance.*

Panditji: Look at the people here. Some come to bathe, washing away the weight of lifetimes. Some come to pray, their lips moving in silent surrender. Others come simply to sit, their eyes searching for something they cannot name. And yet, they all seek the same thing.

For centuries, kings have walked these ghats, warriors have bent their heads in humility, saints have attained enlightenment, and sinners have found redemption. And yet, the river does not judge. She does not ask where you come from or what burdens you carry. She only asks that you surrender—to her, to yourself, to the truth that waits beyond the body, beyond the mind. Ganga is nothing but consciousness.

The boat reaches Assi Ghat, where morning prayers echo in rhythmic waves, blending with the sound of the river lapping against the stone steps. A yogi, clad in saffron, sits in deep meditation near the water's edge, untouched by the world around him. Panditji smiles faintly as he watches him.

Panditji: This is where the great sage Parashurama once rested, where poets have found words that shaped eternity, where those who seek strength in their path come to begin their journey. Strength, not of the body, but of the soul. To renounce, to accept, to bow to something greater than the self—this is where it begins.

(The boat moves on, past ghat after ghat, each holding its own silent story. Tulsi Ghat, where the poet-saint Tulsidas composed the Ramcharitmanas, its very air still carrying the vibrations of those sacred verses. Harishchandra Ghat, where a king once sold himself to uphold his dharma, proving that truth is greater than all riches. Darbhanga Ghat, lined with crumbling palaces, remnants of royal families who once ruled

but have now been swallowed by time. And then, at last, the boat reaches the mighty Manikarnika.)

(Panditji's voice lowers, reverent yet unwavering.)

Panditji: *Yahan aake sab kuch ruk jaata hai. Samay bhi, sharir bhi, sansaar bhi.*

Here, everything stops. Time. The body. The world itself.

This is Manikarnika—the great cremation ground, the threshold between the seen and the unseen. Here, flames have burned for centuries without ceasing. Kings and beggars, saints and sinners, scholars and fools—all are equal before this fire.

It is said that Shiva himself whispers the *Taraka Mantra "Om Nama Shivaya"* —the final truth—into the ears of those who leave their mortal bodies here. This is not death. This is freedom. Kashi is the only place where one can attain moksha simply by dying. And so, people come here not to end their journey, but to complete it.

(The boat slows as the burning pyres come into view, smoke curling into the morning air, carrying the last prayers

of those who have left this world. Yet, in Kashi, there is no mourning. There is only realization. Acceptance. Liberation.)

Panditji: *"Kashi mein jo aaya, woh shiv ka hai. Aur jo shiv ka hai, uska kya chhinn hoga?"*

Whoever comes to Kashi belongs to Shiva. And to one who belongs to Shiva, what can ever be lost?

(He looked around making eye contact with all of us, his voice softer now, but carrying the depth of a thousand years.)

You may have come to Kashi as travelers, but you are not leaving as the same people. Look at the river once more. Feel the wind. Hear the chants rising from the ghats. You are part of something far greater than yourself.

Kashi does not change you. It only reveals what was always within you.

(The boat drifts quietly now, letting the river do the talking. The sun rises higher, casting a golden glow over the city. And in that moment, the passengers realize—Kashi was never just a place. It was a calling. And they had answered.)

This is Bachraj Ghat very sacred for the Jain community who follow non-violence and detachment as part of their faith. Kedar Ghat is named in the belief that Kedareshwar Mahadev is present here. Visiting the temple in this ghat is equal to visiting Kedarnath itself.

Panditji continued, we are going to cross Dashashwamedh Ghat. Yeh sirf ek ghat nahi, yeh Brahmand ka sach hai. This is not a ghat – it is the face of the cosmos itself. This is where Lord Brahma performed the Dashashwamedh Yagna to welcome Shiva. This is where Ganga Aarti lights up in the night, where chants merge with the stars and where every evening the river and sky become one. He pauses for a while, letting us to sink in the significance of this place. The Panchganga ghat is where five sacred rivers once merged into the Ganga, a meeting of forces a confluence of wisdom. Saints still sit here in quiet meditation, knowing that some truths are heard only in silence.

You all must have heard Sage Bhagiratha's story who did penance to bring Ganga to Earth. Bhagiratha was a descendant of King Sagara who undertook a severe penance to bring the celestial river Ganga down to earth to purify the ashes of his ancestors who were cursed by sage Kapila. Moved by his devotion, Lord Brahma granted his request but warned that the force of Ganga's descent would be too powerful for Earth to withstand. Bhagiratha then prayed to Lord Shiva who agreed to catch Ganga in his matted locks. As Ganga descended with immense force, Shiva trapped her in his hair letting her out in gentle streams. This controlled flow allowed Ganga to traverse the Earth finally reaching the spot where Bhagiratha's ancestors lay, thus granting them salvation. This story so many of you know. But few know of those who accompanied Ganga when she came to Earth. They are her tributaries, each carrying a story each with a purpose. I want you all to listen carefully.

The Panditji leaned forward, when Ganga was trapped by Shiva in his locks, he tamed her. But when he released her, she split into many streams and each with a story of its own. "Suchakshu, the river of divine sight, was the first to emerge. It is said that those who bathed in her waters gained clarity—not just of the eyes, but of the mind and soul. Then came Pavini, the purifier, whose waters cleansed not just the body but past karma as well. Hladini followed, bringing bliss to all who touched her gentle waves, as if Krishna's own joy flowed through her."

Panditji's voice rises, full of energy.

"Then there was Nandini, named after the celestial cow of plenty, Kamadhenu. She carried abundance, nourishing the lands and blessing all with prosperity. Ah, and then there was Sita, pure and steadfast, much like Devi Sita herself. It is said that her waters ran deep, silent, and full of untold strength."

He closes his eyes briefly before continuing.

"But wait! Do you know of Savithri? Just as she brought light to the world with wisdom, her namesake river illuminated the souls of those who sought knowledge. And then…"

He pauses dramatically.

"Then came Jahnavi. This was no ordinary river. When Ganga's wild force threatened the hermitage of Sage Jahnu, he grew furious and—imagine this!—drank her up in one mighty gulp!"

The listeners gasp.

"Yes, yes! But Bhagiratha pleaded with him, and out of kindness, Jahnu released her from his ear. From that day on, she became his daughter and was known as Jahnavi."

So you see, Ganga is not alone in her journey. She flows with her sisters, each having a separate story and a purpose.

The boat ride was almost complete, while we were immersed in the narration the boat reached its full length till Namo Ghat and took a turn back towards Manikarnika Ghat.

We were almost done and Nilesh slowly was steering the boat towards the shore.

Ganapathy, fished out some cash as Dakshina for the Panditji.

The Panditji quickly jumped to shore even before the boat could dock and be lashed.

He turned back and looked at us with a pranaam and left.

We slowly got out of the boat and despatched Nilesh. He was done with us. We started walking in those steps of Manikarnika which led to the burning area. We found three bodies cremated and two more in waiting. There was no place to proceed amongst that.

We enquired about the route to take to reach Kashi Vishwanath, and someone pointed us towards a narrow lane. At first glance, it seemed ordinary—just another ancient alleyway in Varanasi, wide enough for four people to walk side by side. But the deeper we went, the more we felt ourselves slipping into a river of human bodies, pulled along by an invisible force. The lane grew denser, and soon, every step required effort. Human traffic flowed both ways, each side inching forward, hesitant yet insistent. We found ourselves caught in a current not of water, but of sweat, breath, and desperation.

The heat pressed in from all sides. Bodies brushed against us, the scent of jasmine flowers from temple vendors mingling with the sharp tang of perspiration. We held onto each other in a single rank, our grips tightening as the flow of people turned into an unrelenting tide. At one point, movement slowed to a crawl. Then, suddenly, it stopped.

Panic. A bottleneck had formed ahead, but those behind us had no idea. They kept moving, pushing forward into an ever-tightening space. The air thickened with unease. Murmurs turned into shouts. The push and pull became a force of its own, a living, heaving beast. We were no longer in control of our movements—the crowd dictated our every step, our very breath.

The shrill blast of a megaphone shattered the tension. A police officer barked orders, but instead of opening the police station gates to relieve the crush, they urged the crowd to keep moving. Common sense would have dictated otherwise, but in that moment, common sense was the rarest thing of all. People clutched at each other, trying to steady themselves amidst the chaos.

Then, as if the gods themselves wished to test our endurance, a deafening chorus of horns erupted. Three two-wheelers, their riders oblivious to the suffocating density, forced their way through the mass of people. The noise was unbearable. Something inside the crowd snapped. A man, driven past his limit, turned and delivered a resounding slap to one of the riders. And just like that, a fight broke out—in the middle of what was already a near-stampede situation.

For a moment, time held its breath. Then, just as suddenly, the fight dissolved, swallowed by the sea of humanity. The current resumed its sluggish flow, and we took baby steps forward, each one an act of faith, an offering to the unseen forces guiding us.

And then, the unthinkable.

A rhythmic chant rose above the din: "Ram Naam Satya Hai." The crowd parted just enough for us to see them—a group carrying two dead bodies, their white shrouds stark against the chaos. They were being taken to Manikarnika Ghat for their final rites. Life and death, side by side, in the same suffocating alley. The ultimate truth woven seamlessly into the fabric of the everyday.

At long last, the path opened up. We gasped for air, our bodies aching, our souls shaken. And yet, as we looked ahead towards Kashi Vishwanath, we saw the endless queue stretching for at least two kilometers. The weight of devotion, the sheer magnitude of faith, pressed down on us. A second thought crossed our minds—was the darshan worth this ordeal?

But then, this was Kashi. The city that strips you bare, tests your will, and yet, calls you forward. And so, we moved ahead, one step at a time.

We all huddled to plan our next step.

Shashank was of the opinion that we should skip it and go back. Both Arya and Sabitha seemed to agree. Ganesh and I were of the mood to send them and we both stand in line for the darshan. We didn't want to miss it after coming all the way to Kashi.

We couldn't decide. We argued but without being able to come to a decision.

I was very steadfast in doing the darshan no matter what.

Sabitha was of the mood to go back and so was Arya and Shashank.

We were all stuck not knowing what step to take next. Each one, stuck to their decision. It was at that time a police constable came to us and asked us, whether our darshan has been completed.

Sabitha with some worried eyes, replied about the level of crowd and about thinking to go back.

The policeman, browsed through his mobile gallery of pictures. There was Sabitha's picture in his mobile.

Is this you madam, he asked.

Perplexed at this, Sabitha asked. Yes, but....

He cut her off and asked all of us to come with him

We followed him.

I went up to him and asked him what was it about and how did Sabitha's picture come to him. I was concerned.

He stopped in front of Gate no 4 which happened to be the main protocol gate.

You can go inside for the darshan, he said.

What, I asked.

Panditji called me and sent me this picture.

I asked him, the Panditji who was in the boat with us.

The police man nodded.

You all just go inside.

He flashed his mobile to the gate security and we were let in smoothly after our pat down checks.

We were inside Kashi Vishwanath mandir. No queue, no crowd and no waiting. From there it took us exactly 15 minutes to finish the darshan and we were out.

We searched for the Panditji within the premises. After what he has done helping us with, we wanted to truly thank him.

We just couldn't find him and with the prevailing security and crowd control it seemed impossible.

We were pleasantly surprised and we were out in all of 45 minutes back to the main market after a beautiful darshan of Lord Kashi Vishwanath.

10

Kashi Vishwanath temple dedicated to Lord Shiva is considered one of the holiest temples of India. It is believed that simple glance of the Jyotirlinga is a soul cleansing experience that transforms life and puts it in a path of knowledge and bhakti. It is a symbol of timeless cultural tradition of highest spiritual values. A visit to Kashi Vishwanath is equal to that earned from visiting the rest of the 11 Jyotirlinga in several parts of India.

---

10 *https://www.templefolks.com/temple-pedia/kashi-vishwanath-temple-varanasi.html*

Har Har Mahadev

We chanted as we walked out of Kashi Vishwanath temple.

With the main temple over so smoothly, we carried out visit of a few more temples and spent most part of the day going around the city while Arya and Sabitha got busy doing some shopping.

It ran in Ganapathy's mind a lot. This is really strange, a Panditji joins us in our boat ride and explains us about the relevance and spiritual nature of the place. Then when we are really troubled to make a decision we are called by the policeman to enter the temple premises bypassing the massive crowd. The Panditji sends a picture, the policeman finds us and ensures that we are let in. I can't believe this happened.

I had this unsettling feeling, but it was too much for me to voice out.

It was around 7 PM by the time we reached the hotel. It was to be our last night at Varanasi. We were to leave for the final leg of our journey to Prayagraj from here.

Around 0930 PM I received a call from Sep Sandip asking for a confirmation as to when we would be reaching Prayagraj the next day. It was the same Sep to Col Murthy had put in a word to help us out at Prayagraj.

Sir, you need to come to Saraswati Ghat sir. He said, he would meet me at the venue.

I told him that I would reach Prayagraj by late evening around 8 PM and beyond and would come to Saraswati Ghat on 7th morning.

Okay sir, he said confirming that he would see me at the ghat at Prayagraj.

We haven't left from Varanasi and our program at Prayagraj was getting streamlined through someone there.

The next day morning, was an easy morning. It was time for us to leave Varanasi for Prayagraj but not before our dip at Ganga. The walk from Ravidas Ghat to Assi Ghat in the pre-dawn hush had its own charm. The streets were just beginning to stir, a few tea vendors already setting up their stalls, the fragrance of boiling chai mingling with the distant echoes of temple bells. The Ganga lay ahead, a vast stretch of water shrouded in a gentle mist, its surface glowing with the first hints of morning light.

We were in high spirits, our chatter and laughter echoing softly against the stone steps as we approached the riverbank at Assi Ghat. The air was crisp, sending little shivers down our spines. But the moment we stepped closer, shoes and slippers discarded, feet meeting the cool, wet sand, a sudden rush of excitement took over. This was it—the legendary dip in the Ganga at the break of dawn. One by one, we waded in, the icy water creeping up our legs like a mischievous prankster, daring us to go further. Sabitha yelped dramatically as the first splash hit their back, sending a ripple of laughter through all of us. The cold was electric, jolting us awake far better than any cup of coffee could. We stood for a second, waist-deep, debating whether to take the plunge. The bravest among us Arya, let out a wild war cry and dove in headfirst, disappearing into the water.

And then it happened. That first dip—the shock of it! Every nerve in the body seemed to light up at once, the chill seizing our breath, making us momentarily forget how to function. But then, as if by magic, the cold stopped being cold. It transformed into something else—something invigorating, something that seeped into the bones and filled us with a deep, inexplicable warmth. The second dip was easier, the third even more so, until we were laughing, splashing, and floating, caught in a moment so perfect it felt timeless. As we dunked our heads under, someone remarked, half in jest, "There go all our sins, washed away in the holy waters!" We laughed, but a quiet part of us believed it, feeling a strange, light sensation as though the weight of countless yesterdays had been lifted.

The river had a life of its own. Tiny ripples played around us, and the morning sun began peeking over the horizon, setting the sky ablaze in hues of gold and orange. The water reflected this celestial drama, turning into liquid fire in some places and shimmering silver in others. A group of locals, clad in dhotis, stood nearby, dunking themselves with rhythmic precision, whispering prayers that mingled with the breeze, reinforcing the belief that this was not just water but something sacred. A few foreign travelers tentatively tested the waters, their expressions a mix of trepidation and delight.

We stayed in longer than we had planned, reluctant to leave the embrace of the river. A boatman rowed past, smiling at our antics, while a few young boys on the steps cheered us on, perhaps amused by our exaggerated shouts every time someone took another dive.

Finally, with the sun climbing higher, we emerged from the water, refreshed, invigorated, and grinning from ear to ear. Towels were pulled out, water dripped off our clothes, and someone jokingly declared that this was better than any spa treatment money could buy. As we sat on the steps, watching the river continue its eternal journey, we realized something—we hadn't just taken a dip. We had played, we had laughed, we had cleansed not just our bodies but perhaps a little of our souls too. The Ganga, in all its flowing grandeur, had welcomed us with open arms, and we had embraced it in return. And for that, we would always come back.

Back at the hotel, Arya and Sabitha decided that they would need to go for some Banares saree shopping.

An eager Tuk Tuk operator volunteered to take them and bring them back. Shashank accompanied the ladies

Our things were packed, Check-out from Hotel Ganga Garden done and bills settled. Ganapathy and I walked towards the jetty at Ravidas Ghat and we sat in those steps watching the Ganga.

A flock of seagulls gathered downstream, their white wings catching the soft glow of the morning sun. They floated effortlessly on the rippling surface, bobbing up and down with the gentle current, before suddenly breaking into motion. One took off first, flapping noisily, and then, as if receiving an unspoken command, the others followed in quick succession. They skimmed just above the water, their wingtips barely brushing the surface, leaving behind tiny ripples that dissolved into the river. Their cries echoed in the morning air, a mix of sharp calls and distant murmurs, as they wheeled in graceful arcs, drawing closer with every pass. The sky above us seemed to come alive with movement, the birds forming fluid patterns, their silhouettes etched against the soft pastels of dawn. Then, in one synchronized move, they descended, gliding low over our heads, close enough for us to hear the soft rustle of feathers. Some hovered momentarily, assessing the humans in their waters, before dipping down, pecking at invisible morsels floating on the surface. The river, the sky, and the gulls seemed to dance together in perfect harmony, a fleeting moment of nature's choreography that left us spellbound, rooted in place, dripping in river water, and grinning in quiet awe.

Ganapathy and I spoke of a lot of things.

As Ganapathy spoke, few things registered in my mind and many things were just passe. I was thinking of something else. Something else which had nothing but questions, infinite questions. Reflections and finally surrendering to not knowing.

It took a while for Arya and Sabitha to finish their sojourn and get back. Our vehicles commenced its wheel roll towards Prayagraj.

The Road to Questions – A Mind Adrift in Kashi

The road stretched ahead, but my thoughts refused to follow a straight path. Varanasi lay behind us, and ahead, the Maha Kumbh. Three out of the four places we had planned to visit were now in the past, but nothing about them felt past. Each city, each experience, had left something unfinished inside me—an echo, a lingering question, a whisper of something just beyond my grasp.

I leaned against the window, watching the Ganga flow alongside us in the distance. The river did not ask where it was going; it simply moved. Its course was never straight, but it was never lost. It swirled, curved, broke apart and rejoined, yet it never stopped moving. And somehow, it always reached the ocean. Was faith like that—an unseen force pulling us forward, whether we understood it or not? Or was that simply another comforting illusion?

Perhaps I was not the traveller here—perhaps I was merely a paper boat in the Ganga, tossed by its currents, carried forward without resistance. But was I drifting toward something, or merely away? Did the Ganga choose its direction, or did it surrender itself to forces unseen? And if the river did not question its course, why did I?

A paper boat is fragile, temporary, insignificant against the vastness of the river. But does its insignificance make it meaningless? Or does its fleeting existence hold something profound? A child sets it afloat with delight, watching it wobble, knowing it will soon be swallowed by the current. The river, indifferent, carries it along, never stopping to ask where it came from or where it will go. Is that not what we all are—paper boats, convinced of our control, unaware that we are always being carried?

We think we choose our paths, that we navigate life with will and reason, but do we? Or are we simply set afloat, believing we steer when in reality, we surrender to something far greater than ourselves? And if I were truly a paper boat, fragile, momentary, what did it mean to float upon the infinite? Was I a witness to something vast—or was I simply dissolving into it?

Naimisharanyam had been the first fracture in my carefully constructed understanding of the world. That bearded old tuk-tuk driver—his words, so casually spoken, had buried themselves in my mind. *"You are searching for something."* Searching? But for what? Faith? Meaning? Or merely an explanation that made sense to me?

I had dismissed it then. But after Ayodhya, after Varanasi, the question refused to let go. I wasn't just witnessing these places—I was being witnessed by them.

It was as if they were showing me something about myself, something I wasn't yet ready to accept.

Ayodhya had been an awakening, a crack in the surface of my mind. The darshan was not just a ritual—it was a collision. The moment I stood before Ram, something beyond reason took over. The collective devotion of millions, the chants that shook the air, the sheer weight of belief—it pressed down on me until I could no longer separate myself from it. I, who had always believed in structure, in plans, in predictability—had let go. And for a brief moment, it had felt… right.

Then came Varanasi. If Ayodhya was devotion sculpted into stone and temple, Kashi was devotion left untamed. It was raw, restless, unfiltered. A place that did not ask for surrender—it simply took. The ghats, each step carved with centuries of longing, told stories not just of saints but of seekers, of wanderers, of those who had come to this city in search of something beyond the self.

At Manikarnika, the flames of the funeral pyres rose without end. The rational mind in me understood its function—the logistics of death, the ceaseless cycle. But the part of me that had stood before Ram and forgotten how to breathe felt something deeper. Was this truly liberation? Or was it simply another layer of the stories we tell ourselves, a way to make peace with the unknown?

I had no answers. Only more questions.

Somewhere between Naimisharanyam's whispered wisdom, Ayodhya's thunderous presence, and Kashi's eternal fire, I had begun to feel like a man staring into a mirror that reflected something I was not yet ready to see. Was I truly searching, or had I been running away from something all along?

And now, the Mahakumbh. The grandest of them all. The confluence of rivers, the confluence of faiths, the confluence of every thought I had carried from one place to the next.

Millions would gather, bathing in the sacred waters, believing that this single dip would cleanse them of lifetimes of karma. Would I find my answer in those waters? Would I even recognize it if I did? Or was this journey not about finding answers, but about surrendering to the questions?

I closed my eyes and imagined myself as a paper boat, its edges softened by water, its path uncertain yet unafraid. But does a paper boat have a choice? Does it fight the river, or does it accept the flow? And what is surrender—weakness, or wisdom? If the Ganga is infinite, and I am merely a fleeting ripple upon its waves, then what is left of me when I am gone?

And what of the river? It swallows paper boats without question, yet it, too, is changing, dissolving, shifting—never the same, never still. What is permanence when even the eternal moves? If Ganga is infinite, and I am part of it, then am I not infinite too? Or am I merely borrowing a moment of its journey?

The river does not hesitate, nor does it mourn the past—it simply flows. And yet, within its boundlessness, there is a paradox: it is at once moving and still, eternal and momentary, vast and intimate.

Perhaps that was the answer—there was no answer. Only the current, carrying me forward. The Ganga was infinite, and I was merely floating upon its surface, light and fragile, yet strangely free. To be a paper boat in the Ganga is to accept that the journey itself is the destination.

For the first time in my life, I did not feel the need to decide. I let go of the illusion of control. I let the current take me. The Ganga is infinite, and I am merely a paper boat upon its waves—uncertain, weightless, yet carried forward nonetheless.

All that is true is human consciousness.

Every road tells a story, some whisper through the rustle of trees, some road through the bustle of cities and some like the road from Varanasi to Prayagraj echo the chants of the past and the quiet introspection of the present. Our journey was supposed to be a straightforward passage, but nothing about these lands is ever just that. Each milestone – Rajatalab, Aurai, Gopiganj, Bhiti, Baraut, Handla, Saidabad and Jhusi was more than a name on a milestone. They were footnotes in an ancient unfolding text.

Shobit slammed the accelerator pedal to the floor and the vehicle was crossing a hundred plus kilometers in the highway eating the miles between us and

Prayagraj. The wheels of our vehicle hummed against the asphalt as we left behind Varanasi. We crossed into Rajatalab, the landscape seemed the change its rhythm as though paying homage to something ancient and unseen. The name itself Rajatalab evoked history, an echo of time when kings and sages understood the most powerful throne was not one made of gold but one placed beside still waters. The Raja Talab (King's reservoir) lay to our right, its darn unhurried waters reflecting the passing sky, shifting clouds and perhaps the unspoken dreams of all those who once stood at its edge. I turned my head as we drove past, feeling an inexplicable pull towards the waters. How many rulers, warriors, sages and travellers had gazed upon this same reservoir, letting its surface reflect not just their faces but the state of their hearts. The story of Rajatalab is more of contemplation.

Once upon a time, the banks of this talab would have seen kings pause their conquests to listen to the whispers of the water. The Kashi Naresh, the revered kings of Banaras, perhaps stood where I now gazed, their royal robes catching the sunlight, their minds burdened with the weight of governance, their souls seeking answers beyond war and wealth. Did they find solace here, in the mirror-like stillness of the water?

I imagined the mahouts guiding elephants down the embankment, their massive feet sinking into the mud, the beasts exhaling deep sighs as they stepped into the cooling embrace of the talab. In the distant past, when the kings of Kashi ruled over these lands, this reservoir would have been more than just a body of water. It would have been a place of judgment and justice, where disputes were settled beneath the banyan trees that still stood, their roots dipping into the soil like veins drawing wisdom from the earth itself.

And beyond the kings, what of the saints? Did some nameless sage once sit here, watching the ripples spread, understanding that life itself was nothing but an expanding circle, moving outward from a single moment? The great Adi Shankaracharya passed through these lands, his words shaping the very philosophy of Advaita. Could he, or another traveler like him, have rested here, allowing the water to dissolve the last traces of doubt before stepping forth to awaken the world?

Rajatalab was no ordinary stop. It was a place where footsteps disappeared but reflections endured.

As our car moved forward, the temple bells in a nearby shrine rang out, their sound dissolving into the wind. Somewhere in those echoes, I felt the past and present intertwine.

How many rulers have built their grand visions here, only for time to erase their names?

The water remembers them.

But just as the sky changes its hues over the reservoir, just as the wind reshapes the ripples, perhaps all things are meant to be washed away—except for those who learn to become the water itself.

I watched the talab disappear in the rearview mirror.

Its whispers remained.

We entered Aurai, a name that carried the hush of legends. There was no grand market, no triumphal arch declaring its significance. Instead it lay silent and unassuming like an old sage who does not speak unless spoken to. But if one listened carefully, if one allowed the mind to quieten, one could hear the whispers of the past, the murmur of stories that have never truly left. It is said that Aurai was once home to a great sage one whose penance was so intense that even the restless winds grew still in his presence. What does it take for the wind, which has never known boundaries, to pause? Was it the weight of his prayers? The gravity of his silence? Or was it simply the unshakable presence of one who had touched something eternal?

The road curved gently, revealing an old banyan tree, its roots thick and gnarled, as if they had spent centuries gripping the earth in meditation. I imagined travelers of another time resting in its shade—merchants from the south, pilgrims from the mountains, ascetics with nothing but a loincloth and a begging bowl.

And yet, what is a pilgrimage?

The word evokes images of barefoot seekers, of chanting devotees walking for miles toward a temple, but isn't every journey a pilgrimage of sorts? We sat in our car, surrounded by the hum of engines, the impatience of traffic, the occasional blaring horn. But weren't we, too, moving with intent? Wasn't there a pull, a reason that made us undertake this road, however ordinary it may seem on the surface?

I wondered—were we any different from those who came before us, or were we simply traveling in a different yuga, following the same quest?

The great rivers have seen all. The sages who walked barefoot, the emperors who rode in gilded chariots, the merchants with their loaded carts, and now, us—in air-conditioned steel and glass, separated from the dust, yet no closer to enlightenment.

Aurai did not ask for recognition, but as we passed through, I felt as though it had marked us. For a moment, I rolled down the window, letting the air rush in. Did the wind truly stop for the sage, or was it waiting for me to listen?

Sitakund at Aurai

The road stretched onward, pulling us away from Aurai and deeper into the heart of Purvanchal, where history and devotion wove themselves seamlessly into the landscape. Fields of wheat and mustard swayed gently in the breeze, and the occasional roadside temple, wrapped in marigold garlands, stood as a quiet sentinel to the unbroken faith of those who traveled this path before us.

As we approached Gopiganj, the very name seemed to hum with something ancient, something timeless.

Gopiganj. The moment it rolled off the tongue, the mind was drawn not to this place, but to a time when the air of Vrindavan was thick with Krishna's flute, when the Gopis danced in a trance, their love so absolute that even the divine had no choice but to surrender.

But history does not place Krishna here. His footprints do not mark the soil of Gopiganj, and yet, his presence was felt in the name itself, in the rhythm of the syllables that seemed to carry a song of devotion.

Did some forgotten bard once stop here on his way to Kashi, singing of Krishna beneath the vast sky? Did a wandering Baul singer, lost in divine longing, leave behind the echoes of his melodies in these lands, carried forward by the wind?

We were moving forward, but Gopiganj made me pause.

Perhaps devotion itself does not require the presence of the divine—it only needs a call, a longing, a remembrance. Was that why the name remained, even when history did not anchor Krishna here?

The road through Gopiganj was smoother than the paths we had crossed earlier, a moment of ease in an otherwise unpredictable journey. And I couldn't help but wonder—was this, too, a metaphor? That in every journey, whether on the road or in life, there are stretches of smooth passage that must be savored, for turbulence is always ahead? That just as Krishna appeared to the Gopis when they least expected but most needed him, moments of grace come in journeys not when we seek them, but when we are ready to receive them?

We passed through Gopiganj quickly, its presence fleeting, but its essence lingering.

Krishna was never here.

And yet, in some inexplicable way, he always had been.

With every passing mile, we were inching closer to Prayagraj, yet the journey was not just geographical—it was a passage through time, through layers of history and devotion.

It was somewhere along this road, perhaps near here, perhaps beyond, that Bharata once walked, his heart heavy with devotion, his steps uncertain yet resolute. Bhiti, this quiet town, lay along the path that once carried the weight of a brother's love and a kingdom's sorrow.

I looked out of the window as we crossed Bhiti, and for a moment, I thought I could feel it—the residue of his grief, lingering in the air like an echo trapped between the past and the present.

Bharata, the brother who never sought the throne, who never desired power, yet upon whose shoulders the burden of Ayodhya had fallen. When Rama was exiled to the forests for fourteen years, Bharata did not celebrate his fortune, nor did he assume the throne with pride. Instead, he walked barefoot to Chitrakoot, across lands like this, begging his brother to return, to reclaim what was rightfully his. But destiny had other plans. Rama refused, and Bharata returned with nothing but Rama's padukas (sandals), placing them upon the throne as a symbol of the true king's presence.

What must that return journey have felt like?

Did Bharata pass through this very land, Bhiti, his heart heavier than his footsteps, his mind burdened by a responsibility he never sought?

Was the wind that brushed against my face the same wind that had once carried his sighs?

I felt a strange kinship with him. What burdens do I carry unknowingly? Are they truly mine, or have they been placed upon me by expectations—by family, by society, by my own unspoken fears? If Bharata, with the weight of a kingdom on his shoulders, could walk in surrender, could I not let go of what I clutch so tightly?

Bhiti was not a place of grand monuments or towering temples. There was no great shrine to remind the world of Bharata's pain. Yet, it did not need one. The land itself held the story, woven into its dust, carried by the silent trees, whispered by the wind.

Our vehicle moved forward, but my thoughts lingered.

Some journeys are measured in miles. Others, in the weight we choose to leave behind.

Beyond Bhiti, the road stretched on, and the world around us seemed to grow quieter. Baraut and Handla came and went, not with the grandiosity of ancient capitals, but with the quiet persistence of places that have always existed and always will.

There were no great temples proclaiming their importance, no ruins whispering of lost dynasties. Instead, there were roadside vendors, old men squatting by tea stalls, children racing each other barefoot, their laughter rising above the hum of passing trucks. Did they know that their everyday existence was a silent defiance against time itself?

In a world obsessed with movement, with ambition, with the pursuit of more, these places did not rush. They lived at their own pace, a rhythm dictated not by the urgency of the world but by the certainty of seasons, of sunrise and sunset, of the simplicity of being.

And I wondered—what is truly forgotten? Places like these, or those who chase an illusion of importance, never pausing long enough to truly exist?

The road continued, the landscape shifting ever so slightly, until we reached Saidabad—the last bend before Prayagraj.

Something changed here. It was almost imperceptible, but I could feel it. The air carried a weight of expectation, the pulse of a city that lay just beyond reach.

And then, as if to remind us that sacred places must be earned, the journey came to a halt. A gridlock. Traffic stretched endlessly ahead, vehicles locked in a slow, reluctant embrace.

I stared ahead at the unmoving road. We were halted just before our final destination—why?

Perhaps it was a reminder that no journey is without its tests. That before one reaches a place of significance, patience must first be learned. That in a world where we are always in motion, sometimes, we must be forced to stop.

Prayagraj was close.

But not yet.

Not just yet.

Saidabad had already tested our patience, but what came next felt like an eternity stretched across a few miles of unmoving metal and frustrated souls. The road ahead, leading into Jhusi, was a river of stalled vehicles, their headlights flickering like exhausted fireflies in the evening haze. We weren't driving anymore—we were crawling, inch by painful inch, into the heart of a city that was already overflowing.

The closer we got, the tighter the gridlock became. And then, as if the universe decided to add another twist to the tale, we saw them—police barricades, their yellow iron frames standing like silent sentinels against the chaos. The policemen, their faces lined with fatigue, waved their arms in mechanical gestures, directing all traffic away from the city's main arteries.

"Phaphamau," they ordered. "Go through Phaphamau."

Phaphamau? Another detour. Another loop in this never-ending spiral into Prayagraj. I exhaled sharply, knowing that resistance was pointless. The city had decided how it wanted us to enter. We weren't in control anymore—if we ever were.

So, we obeyed.

The road to Phaphamau was no better. Another jam. More waiting. The engine hummed impatiently beneath my fingers, but there was nowhere to go. A sea of vehicles stretched ahead, each driver gripping the wheel in resignation, each passenger staring out at the dying light of the day, wondering if they would reach their destination before the night fully took over.

And then, through the tangle of brake lights and stalled movement, the Yamuna emerged below us.

We were on the bridge, the river flowing silently beneath our frustration, oblivious to our human need for urgency. The Yamuna had seen this all before—kings and sages, conquerors and refugees, seekers and sinners. What were we but another fleeting moment in its endless gaze?

I looked to my right, and there it was—the setting sun, a deep, burning orange, dissolving in to the horizon.

For a brief second, the exhaustion faded. The honking, the shouts, the gridlock—they became background noise, insignificant against the sheer beauty of that golden orb sinking into the waters. No matter how long the journey, no matter how delayed the arrival, the sun always sets. And then, it rises again.

More than an hour passed before we finally crept into the city—the chaos of Prayagraj unfolding around us, its veins overworked, its breath heavy with the weight of millions who had come seeking something. The streets swelled with people, the air thick with dust and devotion, the very ground vibrating with the energy of the Mahakumbh.

By the time we reached Civil Lines and checked into our hotel, there was nothing left in us but exhaustion.

No curiosity, no wanderlust—just an overwhelming need for stillness.

We dared not step out into the madness again. Not tonight. Not after what it took to get here. Some journeys demand reflection, and some demand nothing but surrender to sleep.

A quiet dinner at a restaurant within walking distance—a meal more out of necessity than enjoyment—marked the end of our day. Then, back to the room. Doors shut. Curtains drawn. The city outside could wait.

Tonight, there was nothing left to do but sleep.

Ganapathy and I couldn't sleep. Arya and Sabitha, in their infinite wisdom, decided the best cure for our restlessness was a late-night errand—fetching drinking water. We grumbled, of course, but set off anyway.

A small supermarket stood at the end of the street, its shutters halfway down, ready to call it a day. The old shopkeeper peered at us over his spectacles, which precariously balanced at the tip of his nose. With a smile, he agreed to one last transaction.

As he scanned the barcodes, he glanced up. "Where are you both from?"

"Tamil Nadu," Ganapathy replied.

"We came for the Mahakumbh. Heading back tomorrow," he added.

"Ah, that's nice," the old man nodded. Then, with a twinkle in his eye, Ganapathy asked, "Being in Prayagraj, you must be taking a dip at the Sangam every week?"

The shopkeeper chuckled, adjusting his glasses. "In my 78 years, I've bathed in the Sangam exactly three times."

Ganapathy and I exchanged glances. "Three times? That's it?"

"One-third of India comes to Prayagraj for the Kumbh, and you, a lifelong resident, have barely been?" I asked, half in disbelief, half in amusement.

The old man shrugged. "Son, when the river flows through your backyard, you don't always feel the need to jump in. And besides," he grinned, "if a dip alone guaranteed salvation, I'd be selling holy water, not bread and butter."

We laughed, paid for our purchases, and walked back, feeling oddly enlightened.

It was the last day of our week-long trip and today was the reason for which the entire trip was planned. A dip at the Mahakumbh. We were all ready at 05:45 AM and we walked out to the common area where a group of pilgrims were getting together. There was a priest who had come along with them probably taking them around numerous places.

The priest was about to brief them before they left for the Sangam dip. He made all of us chant OM, eleven times. We just joined in with the others. Shobit needed sometime to get ready and we had those extra minutes to hear what the priest was about to say.

[11]The priest commenced his narration to his group. The Kumbh revolves around the story of Samudra manthan or ocean churning which was done by the gods and demons to obtain the nectar of immortality (Amrit). Mount Mandara would become the churning stick and Vasuki acted as the rope. Lord Vishnu himself took the form of Kesava or tortoise and provided the base for the mountain Mandara as everyone feared that it may slip and get submerged into the ocean.

The story is symbolic of the churning of our minds to go deeper into ourselves from where all powers and auspicious things arise, eventually leading to liberation or immortality. The first to emerge in this churning was the venomous haalahala poison which was consumed by Lord

[11] *https://kumbhmela.com/#* (verbatim used with thanks)

Shiva, who upon drinking this poison came to be called as Nilkantha.

The churning continued and then emerged Kamadhenu, Uccaishrava, Choodamani, Kausthubam, and finally amrita kalasa or the pot filled with nectar. Jayanta the son of Indra catching sight of the nectar snatched it from the hands of God Dhanvantari, noticing this Shukracharya, the guru of Demons alerted and the demons chased Jayanta. According to the divine counting, one day of gods is equal to one year of mortal beings and Jayanta kept on running for 12 days to avoid amrita kalasha to fall in the hands of demons.

The four places where Jayanta had put down the amrit kalasha in these twelve years were Haridwar, Prayag, Nashik-Trimbakeshwar and Ujjain, and at these four places at that time the sun, moon,and planets had reached the unique astrological alignment, during which are kumbhmela is held at these places. The nectar pot was saved from the demons by God Brihaspati with the help of Sun, his son Lord Shani and Moon who saved the nectar kumbh from getting damaged.

As mentioned in the Skanda purana, kumbhmela is not just celebrated where the amrit kalasa was put down, but where the nectar had spilled along with putting down of the kalasa. It is believed that these drops gave mystical powers to these places. It is to make oneself gain on those powers that Kumbh Mela has been celebrated in each of the four places since long as one can remember.

The normal Kumbh Mela is held every 3 years, the Ardh (half) Kumbh Mela is held every six years at Haridwar and Allahabad (Prayag) while the Purna (complete) Kumbh mela takes place every twelve years, at four places Prayag (Allahabad), Haridwar, Ujjain, and Nashik, based on planetary movements. The *Maha Kumbh Mela* is celebrated at Prayag after 144 years (after 12 'Purna Kumbh Melas').

Depending on what position the Sun, Moon, and Jupiter hold in that period in different zodiac signs, the venue for Kumbh Mela is decided.

The Astrological aspect of Kumbh is related with traversing planets and stars and their certain alignment. As per the Vedas the Sun is considered as a soul like or life giving. The moon is considered as a lord of Mind. The planet Jupiter or Brihaspati is considered as Guru of Gods. As it takes almost 12 years for Jupiter to transverse to complete zodiac, so the Kumbh is celebrated in accordance at one place after about every twelve years.

"पद्मिनी नायके मेषे कुम्भ राशि गते गुरोः ।
गंगा द्वारे भवेद योगः कुम्भ नामा तथोत्तमाः।।"

When Jupiter enters in Aquarius or Kumbh (zodiac sign) and Sun and Moon in Aries and Sagittarius respectively,Kumbh is held at Haridwar.

मकरे च दिवा नाथे हृमजगें च बृहस्पतौ कुम्भ योगोभवेत्तत्र प्रयागे
ह्यति दूलर्भः
"मेष राशि गते जीवे मकरे चन्द्र भास्करौ ।
अमावस्या तदा योगः कुम्भख्यस्तीर्थ नायके ।।"

When the Jupiter is in Taurus or Vrishabha (zodiac sign) and the Sun and Moon are in Capricorn or Makra, the kumbha is held at Prayag.

। "सिंह राशि गते सूर्ये सिंह राशौ बृहस्पतौ ।
गोदावर्या भवेत कुम्भों जायते खलु मुक्तिदः ।।"

When the Jupiter enters in Leo or Simha (zodiac sign) and the Sun and Moon in Cancer, the Kumbha is held at Nashik and Trimbakeshwar.

"मेष राशि गते सूर्ये सिंह राशौ बृहस्पतौ ।
उज्जियन्यां भवेत कुम्भः सदामुक्ति प्रदायकः ।।"

When Jupiter is in Leo and the Sun and Moon in Aries, the Kumbha is held at Ujjain.

Since Jupiter is in zodiac Simha the Kumbh is held at Trimbakeshwar and Nashik and Ujjain, it is known as Simhastha Kumbh.

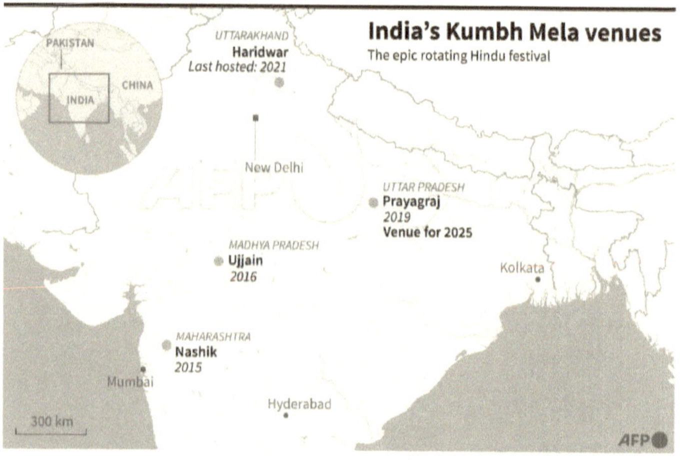

Let us all leave for the Sangam Snaan the priest said. It was a beautiful narration for us too who as passers by was made to stop and listen to the relevance of Mahakumbh. A sort of a briefing before we commenced our journey to Triveni Sangam.

Shobit was ready and we commenced our drive to Saraswati Ghat. It was a smooth drive without any traffic to a fair stretch till we reached the final turn to Saraswati Ghat. There was a police barrier which asked us to divert,

I got down and identified myself and we were duly let in. A few hundred metres drive and we were at Saraswati Ghat. A training area for the army during peace time. I made my first call to Sep Sandip and after a few rings, he picked up. Welcome to Saraswati Ghat sir, he shouted from the other side.

The noise from the diesel engine of the boat was too much for me to hear. But still, I could faintly make out what he said. He was on duty taking another family to Sangam and would be back after two hours, however he has left a permit token at the army kiosk. I identified myself to the Army Jawan at the kiosk and he duly fished out our town from his desk. With a smart salute, he handed over the token to us after which all we had to do was wait for our boat to arrive and take us to Sangam.

It took a full 90 minutes of waiting for our number to be called. There were a few other families whose token numbers were called out. We set sail towards Sangam.

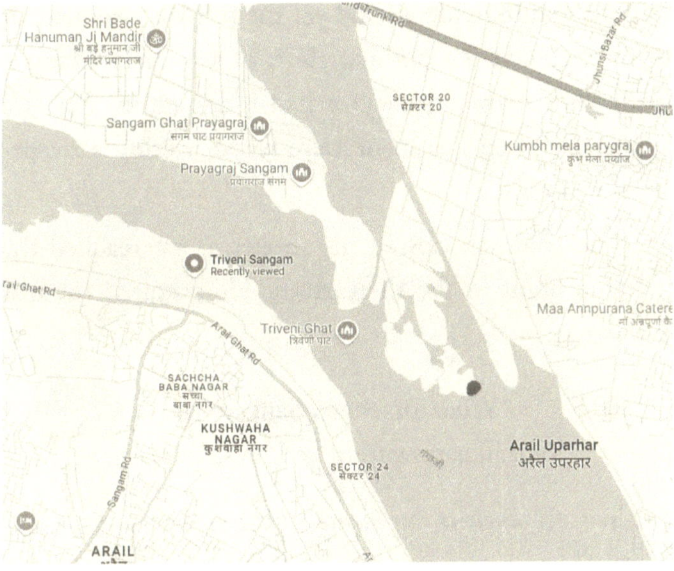

It was a thirty odd minutes sail with the wooden hull cut through the dark waters of the Yamuna. The sun, was a burning orb of bright gold, much above the horizon casting a silvery glow on the river surface. The chants of other pilgrims, the rhythmic sound of the oars dipping into the water, the soft breeze fading into the background, the moment was ours. The moment will be yours only if you feel it without distraction. We reached Sangam, Triveni Sangam, the mighty Ganga with its crystal-clear water and the invisible currents of the Saraswati merging at that very point. The five of us sat close together, the vastness of the place made us feel small. Small in the presence of the something ancient, something as long as time existed and would continue long after us. We had planned the trip to the last detail, every stay, every ticket, minute to minute detail and yet the fact that we made it to the Sangam felt nothing short of a miracle. Had we really chosen this journey or had it chosen us. Had we simply followed a plan or were we answering a deeper unknown calling.

The boatman slowed his strokes as we reached the meeting point of the three rivers. He gestured towards the waters.

"Yahan pracheen Sangam hai,
Yahaan aap swayam ko kho sakte hain.

(This is the ancient confluence, this is where you can lose yourself)

His words struck a chord. Lose ourselves? Or find ourselves.

We climbed down from the boat onto makeshift wooden platforms swaying gently with the currents. The water stretched before us, endless, unbroken, shimmering in the sun. We stood for a moment, silent letting the moment settle into our bones. And then slowly, we stepped in.

The water was cold, but not in an unwelcoming way. It was the cold of something sacred, something untouched by time. The first touch sent a ripple of realization through me—this was no ordinary river, no ordinary dip. This was an immersion into history, into stories, into something larger than anything I had ever known.

I bent down and let the water run through my fingers. How many seekers had stood here before me, doing the same? Had Adi Shankaracharya once cupped this very water in his palms, feeling the weight of its wisdom? Had Bhagiratha, who brought Ganga from the heavens, once looked upon this confluence and known his task was complete? Had some unknown traveler, a nameless pilgrim lost to history, stood here centuries ago, seeking the same clarity I sought now?

I took a deep breath and let myself sink.

For a moment, there was nothing—just water surrounding me, holding me, erasing the noise of the world. In that silence, I was no longer just myself.

I was a thread in a fabric that stretched beyond generations. I was the past. I was the present. I was everything in between.

When I emerged, gasping slightly from the shock of the cold, a sense of lightness took over. Washed away. Cleansed. Not just physically, but in a way I couldn't yet explain.

One by one, the others followed.

I turned to see Sabitha, stepping in gently, closing her eyes as she took her first dip. When she rose, there was a serenity on her face I hadn't seen in a long time. Had she, too, let go of something unseen?

Ganapathy was next. For all his practical, rational outlook, I saw something shift in his eyes as he surfaced. Perhaps faith isn't about belief—it's about experience.

Arya and Shashank followed, their laughter ringing out as they adjusted to the cold. Yet even their joy had a depth to it, as if they, too, felt something beyond the moment.

And then, all five of us stood there, waist-deep in the water, silent.

For the first time in a long time, there was nothing to chase, nothing to prove, nothing to accomplish.

Just us.

Just this.

We had come to Prayagraj for different reasons.

For some, it was curiosity.
For others, it was faith.
For me, it had started as a journey of planning, of logistics, of witnessing the scale of an event—but it had become something else entirely.

Had I come all this way just to see the Kumbh? Or had I come to see something within myself?

Standing in the water, surrounded by my family, I understood.

It wasn't about the Kumbh.

It was about what it did to us.

The Ganga, the Yamuna, and the unseen Saraswati did not care who we were, what our names were, what we had accomplished in life.

They had been here long before us.

And they would be here long after.

All we could do was step in, surrender, and become a part of their story—even if just for a moment.

As we walked back to the boat, dripping and shivering slightly from the cold, I felt something shift within me.

A strange, unexpected peace.

We had reached our destination. And yet, it felt like we were just beginning.

Sitting in the boat, watching the Triveni Sangam fade into the distance, I glanced at my family. We were different now.

Maybe no one else would notice it.

But we would know.

The five of us had left something behind in those waters. And in return, we had taken something with us— something that would stay, long after the journey itself had ended.

And perhaps that was the greatest miracle of all.

As the boatman rowed us back, I looked at the river one last time.

The past had flowed into us.

The present had held us.

And the future awaited.

For the first time, I wasn't in a hurry.

I let the boat drift. As the wooden boat drifted back to Saraswati Ghat, my own paper boat was adrift too.

The boat rocked gently as it drifted over the rippling waters of the Triveni Sangam. The sacred confluence had just embraced us in its timeless waters, washing over our bodies and settling into something deeper—something unspoken. A strange sense of stillness settled over all of us — Ganapathy, Sabitha, Arya, Shashank, and I—as we sat together, the echoes of our dip lingering between us. It was a silence not of exhaustion but of clarity.

An older man, wrapped in a simple shawl spoke loudly, sitting at the edge of the boat, his fingers tracing the rim of the water. He hadn't spoken until now, merely watching the river, as though reading something only he could see. "You have touched the Sangam today," he said, his eyes crinkling in a knowing smile. "But do you know that one of its rivers remains unseen?"

We sat up, drawn in.

"Saraswati?" Arya asked, her voice curious.

The man nodded.

He turned his gaze towards the Allahabad Fort, its walls standing like silent sentinels over centuries of devotion. "Inside that fort, there is a well. They call it Saraswati Koop, for it is believed that deep within its waters, the lost river still flows."

"But if Saraswati disappeared," Shashank asked, "then how can she still exist there?"

The old man smiled. "Who said she disappeared? That which is divine never disappears—it only changes form. Saraswati, the river of wisdom, does not need to be seen to be known. Like true knowledge, she exists even when the eye cannot find her. She flows beneath, hidden from those who seek only with sight, but visible to those who seek with the heart."

I let his words settle over me. Did all sacred things move like this—unseen but never absent?

He continued. "It is said that Akbar, when he built the fort, knew of the well's significance and let it remain untouched.

His fingers trailed through the water, as if tracing invisible lines in the river's current. "Go to that well someday. Stand before it. And close your eyes. If you listen closely, you will hear it.

"And not far from Saraswati's well stands a tree. But not just any tree. A tree that has seen the world end and begin again."

We listened, spellbound, as he turned his gaze towards the sky, where the branches of an unseen banyan seemed to spread into infinity.

Akshaya Vatika: The Tree That Witnessed the End of Time, The Tree that cannot die.

"There was a time when the world ceased to be. The great floods rose, swallowing the earth, dissolving all that once existed into the endless, devouring waters. Oceans raged. Mountains crumbled. The sky and the land became one in the churning void. But in that moment of annihilation, Pralayam, one thing remained—one tree, untouched by the flood, standing above the waters as the last witness of creation."

"The Akshaya Vat?" Sabitha asked, her voice almost a whisper.

The man nodded. "Yes. And beneath its branches, on a lone leaf floating upon the endless ocean, lay a small child—a child with the face of eternity, the cosmic vision of time itself. He sucked the toe of his tiny foot as he lay upon the leaf, unbothered by the dissolution of the world around him. That child was none other than Narayana, the Supreme Being. He lay there, waiting for the world to begin again, the entire universe resting within him, while the Akshaya Vat stood above him, watching over time itself."

Chacha – Are you speaking about Markandeya Charithram that is stated in Srimad Bhagavatham, asked Ganapathy.

Yes, said the old man.

I could see it in my mind—the lone tree, its roots submerged in the endless sea, its branches touching the sky, a small child cradled in the lap of nothingness, waiting for creation to restart.

Ganapathy, usually one for the rational, exhaled deeply. "And it still stands?"

His voice dropped lower. "People go to Akshaya Vat with wishes. They tie threads to its branches, whisper their prayers into its bark. But the true power of the tree is not in granting wishes—it is in reminding us that no matter what happens, some things endure. That we endure."

A hush fell over our small group.

I looked at the river around me, the confluence that had held our bodies just moments ago. And I thought about the stories we had just heard—the invisible Saraswati, still flowing, waiting to be known; the Akshaya Vat, standing in silent witness to all things that come and go.

And then I realized—we were not separate from these stories. Hadn't we, too, traveled all this way, following something unseen but deeply felt? Hadn't we, too, been tested, diverted, halted before reaching Sangam, as if the journey had to shape us before we could be here? Hadn't we, too, stood together, in the confluence of waters, feeling the weight of time and the lightness of surrender?

The old man turned back toward the water, his eyes resting on the horizon. "You are now a part of this.

Whether you realize it or not, the river will remember you. And so will the tree."

It was time to deboard from the boat. We conveyed our thank you to the boatman and left the ghat.

I called Sep Srini and thanked for making it such a smooth experience.

It was another miracle I thought, a chance meeting with Col Murthy at Ayodhya and he having enabled a cake walk sort of a trip in Prayagraj. Amongst the sea of humans who waited for hours caught in traffic and walking miles for a dip, we were at Triveni Sangam at the confluence point making our entire tour to culminate with a lifelong memorable experience.

Another Mahakumbh will never be seen by any of us in our life time and here we were at Prayagraj, at Triveni Sangam, at the confluence point of the three rivers. Blessed …. I thought.

There is no other word other than that.

* * *

The Weight We Carry and the Weight We Let Go

Ganapathy had spent his whole life believing that control was the key to stability. He was the anchor, the one who ensured that life moved in a straight line, free of unnecessary detours. His approach was simple—plan, execute, and adjust if needed. Whether in his career, family responsibilities, or even small things like trips, he found comfort in structure.

But here, standing at the banks of the Triveni Sangam, where the sacred rivers merged into one, he realized—some things were never meant to be controlled. The river, like life itself, had its own current. It could not be grasped, only trusted.

He thought of the paper boat from his childhood—the one he would carefully fold and place on the water, watching it sail until it inevitably sank. He had always focused on keeping it afloat, resisting the current, ensuring it lasted just a little longer. But now, he saw the truth: the paper boat was never meant to last. Its beauty was in the journey, not the outcome.

The river did not ask where it was going. It simply flowed. And maybe, just maybe, so could he. He had spent his life believing that strength lay in holding things together, but what if true strength lay in letting go? As the river lapped at his feet, he imagined himself as that paper boat, surrendering to the current instead of fighting it. For the first time in years, he allowed himself to stand still. No plans, no calculations—just the gentle realization that he, too, could flow.

* * *

The Unseen Rhythms of Life

Sabitha had spent her life in the quiet spaces between others' needs—always listening, always adapting, always ensuring that everything around her remained balanced. It was not a burden; it was instinct. The invisible rhythms of her home, her family, her relationships—they all moved smoothly because she had learned how to keep them so.

But standing inside the temple in Ayodhya, watching the golden glow of the lamps flickering before the deity, she felt something shift. For years, she had been the paper boat carrier—the one who gently placed others on the water, guiding them, ensuring their path was smooth. But had she ever allowed herself to float? Had she ever let the river carry her?

She closed her eyes and let the temple bells ring through her being. In that moment, she understood—nurturing others did not mean she had to neglect herself. She, too, was part of the journey. And like the paper boat, she was allowed to drift, to explore, to exist beyond duty.

She thought of all the small sacrifices she had made over the years, the way she had seamlessly fit into the lives of others without questioning whether she was losing pieces of herself in the process. The river did not question its flow, and for the first time, she decided she wouldn't either. A quiet smile formed on her lips. She didn't need grand changes, no dramatic departures from her life. But she would allow herself small spaces—moments of stillness, time to explore her own joys, the simple act of acknowledging that her happiness mattered too.

As she stepped outside the temple, she felt the evening air wrap around her, whispering something she had always known but never truly embraced—You, too, are worthy of the river's embrace.

***

The Silence Between Words

Arya had always believed in the power of words. A teacher by profession. They were her tool, her shield, her way of understanding the world. She spoke, she debated, she questioned—believing that knowledge and wisdom could always be reached through discourse.

But in Naimisharanyam, as she sat before the old man who recited verses in a voice that carried centuries of devotion, she found herself in unfamiliar territory. There were no explanations, no justifications, no need for debate. There was only the chant, the rhythm, the energy of something she could not name.

For the first time, she did not interrupt. She did not ask. She simply listened.

And in that silence, she felt something shift within her.

She had always feared stillness, believing it was an absence. But now, she understood—silence was not emptiness; it was the space between ripples, the pause before a boat catches the current. The **paper boat does not question the river's path; it simply trusts it**. And maybe, for the first time, she could trust it too.

She thought of all the times she had argued with Ganapathy over trivialities, all the moments she had insisted on explanations from Sabitha, all the times she had dismissed faith as something that needed proof. Yet, here, in this sacred space, proof did not matter. Experience did.

As they walked away from the temple, she smiled to herself. Maybe, just maybe, she didn't always need to have something to say. Maybe, sometimes, the greatest truths were not spoken, but absorbed.

* * *

A Shared Transformation

Each of them had come on this journey with different expectations. Ganapathy, the planner who sought control, had learned that surrender was not weakness but wisdom. Sabitha, the nurturer who had spent her life creating balance for others, had realized that she, too, needed space to embrace her own happiness. Arya, the voice that had always sought clarity through words, had discovered that some answers were only found in silence.

They did not speak of these realizations to each other. There was no need.

Because they had all become paper boats—no longer resisting the current, but allowing themselves to be carried by it.

The journey was still unfolding, but something fundamental had shifted within them. The sacred rivers, the temple bells, the ancient chants—they had whispered something to each of them.

And that whisper, once heard, could never be unheard.

As they neared the end of their journey, they saw the river once more. This time, they did not merely watch it. They understood it. The paper boats they had once been—fragile, uncertain, seeking control—had transformed. They were no longer afraid of where the river would take them.

And as the Ganga flowed, so did they.

A Paper Boat's Journey

Our journey had come to an end with the final dip at Triveni Sangam. From Varanasi, we set out for Lucknow airport, the road stretching endlessly ahead. Each of us carried personal experiences, yet there was a common thread—a connection, an unspoken bond with the places we had visited. The temples, the ghats, the sacred waters, the whispers of the ancient—each moment felt like a divine orchestration.

Some happenings seemed beyond mere coincidence. The last-minute change of dates that unknowingly saved us from a stampede. The unexpected meeting with the baba at Naimisharanyam. The darshan at Ayodhya that felt like gazing upon the divine itself. The serendipitous encounter with Col. Murthy, who arranged our Sangam snaan. The boat ride at Guptkar Ghat. The priest who narrated the story of Kashi as we drifted on the river. The sudden appearance of a policeman who cleared the way for a smooth darshan at Kashi Vishwanath. And the Sangam dip, entwined with the legends of Mahakumbh, Saraswati Koop, and Akshay Vatika.

Could these truly be coincidences?

Coincidences don't occur with such precision over an eight-day journey. Each day unfolded like a chapter, setting the stage for the next. Obstacles dissolved as if guided by an unseen hand. As I sat in the front seat, head resting on the car seat, eyes closed, the past days replayed in my mind—beautiful, yet unsettling. My subconscious whispered:

It was something else.

The river flows.

It always has. Long before we named it, long before we could comprehend its vastness, the river has been flowing. The Ganga is not just a river, it is a witness, a silent observer to all that comes and goes. In its endless movement, it mirrors the flow of human consciousness, the eternal witness within us, untouched by time, yet experiencing everything. We, like paper boats, are set adrift upon its water, carried forward by unseen currents. Some boats sail smoothly, others capsize at its first ripple. But the river remains – watching, carrying, receiving.

As I stood at the Triveni Sangam, watching the Ganga, Yamuna, and the unseen Saraswati merge, a thought surfaced—where does one river end and the other begin? What is separate? What is one? In that confluence, I saw my own mind, my struggles, the pull of the material, and the whisper of the infinite. The chase for meaning, for identity, for belonging—all dissolving in that great merging.

Mahavishnu is the forest. The spirit of Naimisharanyam breathes through the trees, a silent pulse of the divine, reminding us that what we seek outside is already within. The sages knew this. They gathered in that sacred space not to escape the world, but to understand it, to witness the silent consciousness that pervades all.

Lord Ram is not just a prince, nor a god confined to the temples we build for him. He is human consciousness in its purest form—the dharma that calls us, the path that demands sacrifice, the devotion that ties love and duty as one. His exile is our exile, the distance we feel from our true selves. His return is the promise that one day, we too will find home within.

And Shiva, the stillness amidst chaos, the dance of destruction and rebirth—he whispers a truth that only silence can hear. The ashes on his skin are the remnants of all that was, the reminder that nothing truly stays. He does not chase the world, yet the world moves within him. He is time, he is eternity, he is the answer to every question the troubled mind has ever asked. And perhaps that is why he meditates—because the answers were never meant to be spoken, only realized.

I think of the *Mandukya Upanishad*, of the *Na pragyam* shloka that speaks of what is beyond waking, dreaming, and deep sleep:

नान्तःप्रज्ञं न बहिष्प्रज्ञं नोभयतःप्रज्ञं न प्रज्ञानघनं न प्रज्ञं नाप्रज्ञम्। अदृष्टमव्यवहार्यमग्राह्यमलक्षणं अचिन्त्यमव्यपदेश्यमेकात्मप्रत्ययसारं प्रपञ्चोपशमं शान्तं शिवमद्वैतं चतुर्थं मन्यन्ते स आत्मा स विज्ञेयः॥

Nāntaḥ-prajñaṁ na bahiṣ-prajñaṁ nobhayataḥ-prajñaṁ na prajñānaghanaṁ na prajñaṁ nāprajñam, adṛṣṭam-avyavahāryam-agrāhyam-alakṣaṇam-acintyam-avyapadeśyam-ekātma-pratyaya-sāraṁ prapañcopaśamaṁ śāntaṁ śivam-advaitaṁ caturthaṁ manyante sa ātmā sa vijñeyaḥ.

This verse speaks of *Turiya*, the fourth state of consciousness beyond waking, dreaming, and deep sleep. It is not internal or external awareness, nor is it both. It is not mere knowledge or ignorance. It cannot be grasped by the senses or described in words. It is the cessation of all worldly projection, the peace beyond understanding, the auspicious, the non-dual. This is the Self, the ultimate reality that must be realized. It tells us that the mind's relentless search for answers—through logic, through experience, through observation—will always fall short. The true nature of consciousness is beyond definitions. It is not something to be attained, but something to be realized. Like the river that simply flows, it does not need to prove its existence. It just is.

This realization brings us back to the great spiritual centers—Naimisharanyam, where Mahavishnu exists as the eternal forest, whispering the wisdom of sages through its rustling leaves. It is here that consciousness unfolds itself in its most primal and natural form, uninterrupted by the constructs of society.

Lord Ram, the embodiment of dharma, teaches us that consciousness is not a static force but a journey—an exile and a return. He walked the forests, lived through trials, and emerged with a truth that is universal: the self is realized not in comfort, but in experience. Just as he reclaimed his rightful place in Ayodhya, so too must we reclaim our inner awareness.

Shiva, in his meditative stillness, is the very essence of *Turiya*. He sits beyond the constructs of time, untouched by waking, dreaming, or deep sleep. His third eye sees beyond illusion, reminding us that what we perceive is only a fragment of reality. His dance of destruction is not chaos, but transformation—the breaking of illusion to reveal the eternal.

And at the Triveni Sangam, where three sacred rivers meet, we see the convergence of all these truths. The physical merging of the Ganga, Yamuna, and Saraswati is but a reflection of the merging within us—the dissolution of ego, the acceptance of impermanence, and the embrace of the infinite. Just as the waters flow together into one, so too must we surrender to the greater consciousness, dissolving our false boundaries and realizing the oneness that has always been.

The troubled mind, the restless spirit—it seeks answers in the world, in accomplishments, in possessions, in fleeting moments of pleasure. But as the fields rolled past our car window, I realized something profound. The paper boat that fights the river will only tear apart. But the one that surrenders, that understands the impermanence of each ripple—such a boat will see the ocean.

Our journey was never just about places, temples, or rituals. It was about returning—to the self, to the silence that has always been there. In this age of noise, where we drown in distractions, there is something radical about stillness. There is something revolutionary about realizing that the true self is not in the race, but in the witness.

I set my paper boat upon the Ganga once more in my mind.

I watch it drift, knowing it will not last forever. And yet, in that fleeting moment, in that gentle surrender to the river's will, there is a beauty that words cannot hold. The boat may dissolve, but the river remains. The body may fade, but consciousness is eternal. But what is surrender? Is it the acceptance of fate, or the ultimate realization of one's true nature? If all of existence is but a ripple in the vast stream of time, then where does time itself flow? Is enlightenment the dissolution of self, or the full awareness of self? If we are all part of the same current, why do we feel so separate? And if all paths lead to the same ocean, does the journey itself matter?

I do not have the answers.

As our car neared the airport, I closed my eyes and listened to the hum of the tires against the road. The river speaks, all you need to do is to listen in the silence.

And in that whispering stillness, I hear the river ask—

"Will you ever know?"

And in that whispering stillness, as our car neared the airport, I heard the river say —

"Let go."

JAI SHRI RAM